*Theology* 1977     1.95

# A Time to Remember:
# BEGINNINGS

## Edited by Barry L. Callen

*Church of God Heritage Series*

**Published By
Warner Press, Inc.
Anderson, Indiana**

*The publishers gratefully acknowledge the help of authors and publishers who permitted their work to be reprinted in this volume. Copyright notices appear with the appropriate selections.*

# TABLE OF ENTRIES

*Spreading the Message*

*The Message Takes Root*

# INTRODUCTION

**EVEN THOUGH** Christians always have believed that truth ultimately will triumph, they have had to face a persistent and frustrating reality: At each stage along truth's path to this final victory there are limiting factors to be faced. One way to identify these factors in a general way is simply to state that we limited human beings seek to comprehend and appropriate God's revelation in the crippled context of a world corrupted by sin.

Although we often wish that it were not as true as it is, the fact remains that the value system, cultural assumptions, and political and economic arrangements of each human society have a significant influence on the attitudes and preoccupations and general manner of life of the people in that society. Usually even the religious convictions and practices that prevail in a particular setting do not remain free of the shaping pressures of their immediate surroundings.

Those persons who believe in God most deeply and have been freed most fully by the power of the new creation available in Christ tend to be very aware of and dissatisfied with the domination of stale traditions, self-satisfied intellectuals, powerful personalities who manipulate the masses, and popular prejudices that bind and belittle people. And, for such Christians who long to function in an atmosphere saturated with openness to God and obedience to his will, there is a further frustration. There is that maze of historic church creeds and complex church organizations which have their own tendency to look and function in mechanical ways much more related to the non-church world than to what the New Testament seems to teach.

But there may be an alternative to such multiple frustrations. In a given time and among a dedicated group of serious and searching Christian people, God may choose to act on behalf of their desire to escape the restrictive establishments of their time in favor of a unique perception of truth and a pattern of life styled by God just for them. While such special divine activity must still be received by fallible persons and applied experimentally in unfavorable circumstances, it remains true that these divinely-given opportunities do come and, when they do, there always is someone who senses their presence and seeks to obey. So long as this is so, there is hope that we Christians are not mere captives of our times and blind tools in the hands of our own ignorance and prejudice. God still lives and acts. Despite all, God's own people will continue the quest to rediscover their own divine birthright. Truth will triumph!

In this volume our attention is focused on one particular group of Christian people who have come to be known as the "Church of God Reformation Movement." These people were very much a part of the American social and religious scene in the latter part of the nineteenth century. Because of their fresh vision of Christian truth and their courageous commitment to it, inevitably they came into conflict with that world. The vision emerged within various individuals and then began to adhere into a corporate conviction that God was showing them a better way. Despite misunderstanding and opposition and with a distinct lack of significant numbers of persons, amounts of money, or supporting organization, they were persistent and effective in championing their vision of this truth from God and of its dramatic implications for the life and work of his people. They were sensing the possibility of a triumph of truth in their very midst.

The intent in these pages is to present selected portions of representative materials which identify the setting and tell the story of this particular group of Christian people. In order to understand the context in which this movement took its rise, the first section of this initial volume presents materials not authored by members of the movement in question, but by competent Christian scholars of related traditions whose insights provide a framework in which the movement can engage in helpful self-criticism. It is both inevitable and right that the movement should look back and come to some conclusions about the issues faced and the answers offered by such a previous generation of their own visionary Christian leaders. And, in order to do so with adequacy, a wide variety of perspectives needs to be considered. Fortunately, for a people who have chosen to be open to all truth, there is a readiness on the part of this particular movement to research all relevant information with a reasonable degree of openness and objectivity.

The bulk of the materials that follow are authored by prominent persons from within the movement who have described those early events and central issues which first brought the movement into existence. Included are selections that elaborate with vividness and detail the means by which this movement began to spread and the circumstances related to its taking root in various parts of the United States and throughout the world.

The early leaders of this movement expressed their vision in dramatic and varied ways. It was believed to have been a time of "evening light" in which they had "seen the Church" and had dared to "come out of Babylon." In short, they felt freed to step beyond the obvious limitations of the Christian world of their time into the fuller reality that God intended and enabled. They were both humble and bold as they submitted themselves to the glorious realities of Christian experience which suggested the possibility of a whole new epoch for the Church. It amounted to the birth of a new reformation. Our immediate concern is to understand how it all began.

Barry L. Callen
Anderson, Indiana

# Dramatic Social Change

## by

### Timothy L. Smith

Excerpted from *Called unto Holiness* (Kansas City, Mo.: Nazarene Publishing House, Copyright © 1962). Used by permission.

**THE AMERICAN** Civil War, lasting from 1860 to 1865, ushered in a new era in our nation's history. An urban and industrial society rapidly replaced the simple agricultural environment in which Thomas Jefferson and the author of the McGuffey readers had lived out their days. Commerce and manufacturing lured hundreds of thousands of young people from the farms of the Old World and the New. In the cities and towns, these newcomers often lived in miserable, disease-ridden hovels. They endured periodic unemployment and faced multiplied temptations to drunkenness and vice. Roman Catholic immigration entirely changed the complexion of cities like Boston, Lowell, Pittsburgh, Cleveland, and Chicago. Barriers of language and religion only complicated the bloody strife which soon broke out between wage earners and employers.

Farming, meanwhile, became a speculative enterprise. The new machines which Cyrus McCormick turned out encouraged immigrants and native-born Americans alike to go west to seek their fortune. Millions of acres beyond the Mississippi were laid to the plow. Overproduction and chronic depression resulted, heightening rural suspicions of the wealthy and creating a new sectional discord, West and South against the urban East. Feelings reached white heat in the middle 1890s, when William

9

# A Time to Remember: BEGINNINGS

Jennings Bryan, the "Boy Orator" from Nebraska, first ran for the presidency.

As the twentieth century came on, the effects of the industrial revolution appeared more sweeping still. The farm-to-city movement became a torrent. Though federal law tended to restrict Catholic immigration from southern and eastern Europe, Dixieland Negroes now moved in large numbers upon Detroit, Chicago, Indianapolis, New York, and Philadelphia, creating grievous tensions. Meanwhile, mass education and the allurements of city life quickened the pace by which young people threw off parental restraints and discarded old values. The daily newspaper, the popular magazine, the moving picture theater, and the automobile, radio, airplane, and television each in turn increased the passion for movement and distraction. They spread novel ideas and made tragedy and scandal the chief topics of thought and conversation. On another level, the new university graduate schools at Harvard, Yale, Johns Hopkins, and Chicago popularized theories about man's origin and nature, his social relations, morals, and religion which challenged the older Christian outlook. Their departments of physics and chemistry turned out white-robed scientists and technicians who soon replaced the black-garbed clergy as the recognized experts on the good life.

That the churches were all this while falling under the spell of wealth and power did not make the task of holiness preachers any easier. Denominational executives imitated the methods of business tycoons in building up the strength and income of their organizations. Local congregations neglected spiritual matters to pander to the social wants of their people. In the seminaries, to be sure, earnest men grappled with the new learning and the ethical issues which urban poverty and industrial strife had raised. The new faith of modernism which they brought forth was deadly serious about righting social wrongs. But it rejected the ancient doctrines and the old-fashioned revivals which hitherto had made the war on sin effective. The masses of churchgoers either misunderstood or suspected it. To most laymen, the "social gospel" seemed nothing more than a sanction to church festivals and Sunday school dances. The shallow faith prevailed that education, democracy, and liberal Christianity were soon to usher in earth's most glorious age.

# Sectism on American Soil

## by

### Charles Clayton Morrison

Excerpted from pp. 4-6 of *The Unfinished Reformation* (New York: Harper and Row, Publishers, Copyright © 1953). Used by permission of the publisher.

**OUR AMERICAN** soil has seemed to provide an ideal spawning ground for the proliferation of sectarian churches beyond anything known elsewhere in Christendom. How shall we account for this unique phenomenon? I suggest three possible explanations.

1. The principle of religious liberty guaranteed by our Constitution tended to be carried over from the political sphere to the sphere of religion, that is, from the state to the church. This psychological transference was more or less unconscious. The neutrality and impartiality of the American state toward all forms of religion subtly predisposed Protestant people to assume that the creation of a new denomination was not only legally irreproachable but could be religiously approved. "This is a free country, isn't it?" became the colloquial justification by which the withdrawal of a disaffected group to form a new denomination was appreciably relieved of any moral or religious reproach. James Madison who, more than any other statesman, was responsible for the First Amendment, had said, "The more independent religious bodies, the more secure would the government be in its freedom from church influence." The Protestant mind easily, though fallaciously, tended to assume that if this multiplication of denominations was good for the government it was also good for religion. Sectarian diversity

11

was therefore accepted as an ecclesiastical virtue and any Christian inhibition on further division was not seriously felt.

2. A denomination from whose membership a disaffected group threatened to secede was in no position to present an effective religious reason why it should not do so. The parent denomination itself had originated in essentially the same kind of situation as that which it now confronted in the threatened secession of its own children. With what consistency, therefore, could the parent now chide her children for doing what she herself had done a century or two centuries or three centuries ago?

When we view the whole history of Protestant denominationalism, it appears as a long series of schismatic chain reactions—one schism producing other schisms and they in turn producing others, in a process which continued up to, let us say, the late nineteenth century. Prophets of church unity periodically appeared throughout this history who endeavored to arrest this chain reaction, but their valiant efforts were futile. The denominational system was generally regarded as established, as a normal expression of Protestantism.

The individualism of the time and of the country provided a favorable environment for the proliferation of denominations. It also provided an unfavorable environment for Protestantism to think in terms of the church catholic. The church, as church, had virtually passed out of the Protestant mind which was now preoccupied with the churches. The church catholic had become the church invisible, a transcendental or spiritual entity, not a historical and empirical entity. There was no conceivable limit to the number of denominational churches which could legitimately arise. The creation of one more denomination by secession from an existing denomination could hardly be conceived as violating any fundamental Christian principle. Indeed, it was implicitly assumed and often explicitly argued that the rivalries among the denominations would stimulate and intensify the spiritual life of all the churches, to the benefit of Christianity as a whole. This result would follow in much the same manner as *laissez-faire* competition in the economic order was supposed to produce a net result of harmony and the maximum welfare of all.

3. Another factor explaining the uninhibited spawning of so many denominations on American soil may be found in the psychology of the frontier. Until modern times, the American people have always lived on the frontier. Geographically, it was an ever-moving frontier, and behind its advancing border there was going on a progressive consolidation and stabilization of political, cultural and religious institutions. But even so, the frontier psychology remained after the frontier had passed on. This was the dominant characteristic of the American spirit, not only in the newer west but in the older east. It took the form of a lusty independence, a distinct feeling of having broken with the past. In this New World the people now confronted not only the opportunity but the necessity of fashioning new institutions with only a dim reference to the past and to the Old World. Thus the continuities of history were appreciably severed and the sense of loyalty to a heritage whose values should be conserved was dimmed. This spirit of self-sufficiency and independence pervaded the whole political, cultural and social life of the people. It also pervaded their religious life.

Naturally, the concept of the church catholic, the universal church of history, could hardly be assimilated by a mentality conditioned by such an environment. It would seem vague, unempirical and irrelevant. The church, as church, was indeed a reality, but hardly a historical reality. It was an invisible and transcendental reality. The denomination had taken its place.

# The First "Come-Outers"

### by

### Timothy L. Smith

## A Time to Remember: BEGINNINGS

**THE HOLINESS** movement was born of great revivals. It prospered from the newly employed energies of laymen and women preachers. And it was in large measure centered in the cities. Urban pastors and evangelists who ranged freely over two continents, rather than rude frontiersmen, gave the awakening its original impetus and direction. The rural surroundings in which camp meetings and summer conferences took place could not hide the fact that most of the leaders and participants were city dwellers. The tented grove provided a welcome refuge from the city's anxiety and tumult.

Nevertheless, as we shall see in a moment, the rapid pace of social change soon created conditions in urban Christianity which led to a conflict over holiness. The increase of wealth and social pretension in city congregations of humble origin did not fit the pattern of perfectionist piety. Nor did the new goals by which church administrators planned their work. The outcome, after a brief struggle, was the organization of a dozen new Wesleyan denominations, of which the Church of the Nazarene was to become perhaps the most significant.

Why did the holiness revival lead to the organization of independent churches, despite the frequent pledges of loyalty which its leaders made to the older denominations? The answer to this question is by no means simple, but it is fascinating.

By 1885, the sweep of the awakening into the Midwest and South was producing two more or less distinct groups. One, largely rural, was more emotionally demonstrative, emphasized rigid standards of dress and behavior, and often scorned ecclesiastical discipline. The other was urban, intellectual, and somewhat less zealous about outward standards of holiness. Its leaders were eager for alignment with all in the older churches who would share their central aims.

Those who earliest left the church came from the first group. Members of the more conservative party withdrew only under great provocation. Many of them lived and died in the church of their fathers. This was true of the Boston leaders especially —Daniel Steele, William McDonald, Charles J. Fowler, and Bishop Willard F. Mallalieu—as well as of Henry Clay Morrison of Kentucky and J. O. McClurkan, of Nashville,

Tennessee.

Four factors entered into their decision to stay or leave: (1) the persistent opposition of ecclesiastical officials to independent holiness associations and publishing agencies; (2) the recurrent outbursts of fanaticism among persons who were members of the associations but not of the churches; (3) the outbreak in the 1890s of strenuous attacks upon the doctrine of sanctification itself; and (4) the increasing activity of urban holiness preachers in city mission and social work.

In all cases, however, as we shall see in a moment, the exodus was intermittent and disorganized. Independent bands and congregations arose in response to local situations. They usually included persons who formerly belonged to several different communions. And they coalesced slowly and rather haphazardly into organized denominations.

A series of premature secessions which extremists provoked in the Middle and Far West around 1880 seriously complicated the relations of the holiness movement to the churches. It put the more responsible leaders on the defensive, forcing them to profess full loyalty to the older denominations during the very years when official but covert resistance to their doctrines was reaching the danger point.

The careers of four men illustrate this story well. Daniel S. Warner founded the Church of God (Anderson, Indiana) in 1880. Hardin Wallace paved the way in Texas and California for the Holiness church. John P. Brooks, editor for the Church of God (Holiness), formulated the theory of "come-outism." The fourth, S. B. Shaw, of Lansing, Michigan, tried but failed to bring about a national holiness union which he hoped would bypass the church question entirely.

D. S. Warner's Church of God carried the nonsectarian traditions of the holiness revival to such extremes that he rejected entirely the idea of an organized denomination. Local congregations kept no membership records and were bound to others only by the fellowship of the Spirit. The founder believed that he was commissioned to unite all Christians on the basis of Jesus' prayer recorded in the Gospel of John, chapter seventeen, "Sanctify them . . . that they all may be one."

Warner's wife was the earliest to fall by the wayside. She announced in 1884 that she was "thoroughly convinced that this effort to unite God's people by calling them out of the churches is not God's plan of unity." It simply "cuts off a few by themselves, who get the idea that none are clearly sanctified unless they see as 'we' do." Although Mrs. Warner professed her love for all who were associated with the movement and especially for her husband, she deplored their surrender to "the same self-righteous pharisaical spirit" which "Christ rebuked and denounced when he was here on earth." Absurd fanaticisms, she noted, were already cropping out here and there.

Nevertheless, Warner's concept of the church appealed to a widespread suspicion of ecclesiastical machinery. The Church of God has persisted into the twentieth century to become one of the stronger of the small holiness denominations. It maintains a college and publishing house at Anderson and carries on an extensive missionary enterprise.

# Disruption over Holiness

## by

### Richard Quebedeaux

From *The New Charismatics* by Richard Quebedeaux. Copyright © 1976 by Richard Quebedeaux. Reprinted by permission of Doubleday and Company, Inc.

**A CLOSE KINSHIP** exists between Pentecostalism and the Holiness movement from which it emerged. Holiness as a movement was an outgrowth of "perfectionist" teaching and revivalism both before and after the Civil War. Its development was greatly facilitated by certain Methodists (and others) who revived a faded interest in John Wesley's doctrine of sanctification (Christian perfection) neglected in Methodism by that time; and although the movement grew largely under Methodist leadership, it actually operated on an interdenominational basis—to stimulate religious piety as an antidote for the ''worldliness'' thought to prevail in an ''apostate'' institutional church. In this connection, Prudencio Damboriena, a Roman Catholic scholar, puts forward five basic reasons for the evolution of the Holiness-Pentecostal movement in the late nineteenth and early twentieth centuries. These include (1) an apparent departure from ''the true faith'' in the historic churches (signaled by their increasing acceptance of Darwin's evolutionism, Kant's rationalism, Schleiermacher's religion of experience, Bushnell's theories on Christian nurture, and Rauschenbusch's Social Gospel); (2) the dead formalism of the established denominations; (3) the pervasive worldliness in the churches, especially in Methodism, where separation from the world was by then a dead issue, and in which traditional prohibitions—from card playing to drinking—had been rescinded; (4) the substitution of personal religion by mere knowledge and external profession; and (5) the resistance of endorsement of urgently needed reforms by denominational hierarchies.[1]

William Boardman, an American Presbyterian, and Robert Pearsall Smith conducted Holiness meetings in England that resulted in the famous Keswick interdenominational conferences for the deepening of spiritual life. In America, the Holiness movement was greatly aided by the use of media fast disappearing in the established churches—revival campaigns, camp meetings, and inexpensive printed literature. Its theological thrust was the belief that when the Holy Spirit makes his abode in the heart, it will be evidenced by a definite emotional experience—a ''second blessing,'' Spirit baptism.

Because of mainline ecclesiastical opposition, recurrent outbursts of fanaticism among Holiness fellow travelers, increasing attacks on the Holiness doctrine of sanctification, and the growing activity of urban Holiness preachers in city missions and social work, it became expedient for these Holiness bands to withdraw from the already established churches and form their own denominations—such as the

Church of the Nazarene, Church of God (Anderson, Indiana), and the Christian and Missionary Alliance.[2]

# Radical Holiness Movements

### by

### Timothy L. Smith

Excerpted from *History of American Methodism,* ed. by Emory Stevens Bucke (Copyright © 1964 by Abingdon Press).

**WHAT IS** often overlooked is that this optimistic belief in man's perfectibility by grace was the contribution Methodists made to the romantic idealism which underlay so much of the movement for social reform in the late nineteenth and early twentieth centuries. It was fully as important as the "progressive orthodoxy" being taught at Andover Seminary during these years. It required, moreover, no break with the denomination's heritage. Wesley's followers could and in many cases did embrace the emerging social idealism without rejecting their founder's message. Ethical earnestness, a belief in the immanence of God's sanctifying spirit, a readiness to accept the call to consecrate oneself and one's resources to the Kingdom of God, and an unreserved acceptance of the law of love—these were as much the hallmarks of the new social Christianity as they had been the foundations of old-time Methodist religion. To this fact William and Catherine Booth, leaders of the Salvation Army, gave unforgettable testimony. Zeal for personal holiness, to be sure, pulled some men into isolation from social needs; but the larger number found service and sacrifice for humanity the essence of the divine compulsion

---

[1]Prudencio Damboriena, *Tongues As of Fire: Pentecostalism in Contemporary Christianity* (Washington, D.C.: Corpus Books, 1969), pp. 29-30.

[2]Damboriena, *Tongues As of Fire,* p. 24.

they called perfect love.

As tihe passed, however, a growing cleavage separated the denomination's official leaders from those who made a specialty of the second blessing. The tension stemmed in part from the rise after 1875 in the Midwest and South of a rural and more radical phase of the holiness revival. A company of evangelists appeared who were seemingly more intent upon Puritan standards of dress and behavior than on perfect love, and certainly less attached to Wesleyan tradition and discipline. Several independent sects emerged with their blessing, long before the crisis of the 1890s drove many of the older and more urban "loyalist" party out of the church.

Typical of the radical leaders was John P. Brooks, editor of *The Banner of Holiness,* published in Bloomington, Illinois. Although at first a loyal Methodist, Brooks left the denomination about 1885. Two years later he published *The Divine Church,* an attack on organized denominations which became a textbook of "come-outism" from that day onward. Brooks was by that time editing *The Good Way,* a magazine published by the group in Missouri and Kansas which later adopted the name Church of God (Holiness). Another such figure was Daniel S. Warner, who founded the Church of God, with headquarters in Anderson, Indiana, in 1880, on an antidenominational platform. Hardin Wallace, an Illinois evangelist, initiated the holiness camp meeting and "band" movement in rural east Texas in 1877, then went on to southern California to lend inspiration to what later became the Holiness Church. S. B. Shaw, of Lansing, Michigan, after several unsuccessful attempts to unite the radical wing of the movement in that state on a nondenominational basis, formed a short-lived sect of his own known as the Primitive Holiness Mission.

# Results of Revivalism

by

## Williston Walker

Excerpted from *A History of the Christian Church* (New York: Charles Scribner's Sons, Copyright © 1918). Reprinted by permission.

**THROUGH** the revivals, through missionary organizations and voluntary societies, an evangelistic, pietistic interpretation of Christian faith became widely disseminated in America in the nineteenth century. The denominations that employed the revival pattern most fully grew to be the giants in this period of national expansion. Methodists, a scant fifteen thousand strong at the time of their independent organization in 1784, were well past the million mark by 1850. The Baptists, about one hundred thousand in number at the opening of the century, had increased eightfold by the mid-century mark. Congregationalists and Presbyterians, among whom the nineteenth-century revival had appeared so early, continued to gain from the awakening, but internal resistance in both bodies to revival emphases inhibited them, and they fell behind in comparative denominational strength, dropping from the commanding place they had held at the dawn of the century.

The Presbyterians were also torn by controversy. Those, often of Scotch-Irish background, who held firmly to confessional standards and to traditions of an educated ministry were sore troubled by frontier revivalists whose doctrinal emphases and ordination standards were more lax. Attempts to curb them, however, led only to schism. In 1803, Barton W. Stone (1772-1844) led a group of evangelistic Presbyterians out of the Synod of Kentucky. These "New Lights" soon dropped all "sectarian" names, seeking to be known simply as "Christians." Several years later, attempts to discipline Cumberland (Kentucky) Presbytery revivalists led to open break, and the formation of what became the Cumberland

Presbyterian Church. Some of the smaller Presbyterian bodies suffered schism too. Thomas Campbell, a Seceder Presbyterian minister in the north of Ireland, came to America in 1807, and began work in western Pennsylvania. Here his freedom in welcoming Presbyterians of all parties to communion aroused criticism, and he was disciplined by the Seceder Presbytery of Chartiers. Campbell felt it his duty to protest against such sectarianism, and to assert as the standard of all Christian discipleship the literal terms of the Bible alone, as he understood it. Thomas Campbell now broke with the Seceder Presbyterians, but continued to labor in western Pennsylvania, announcing as his principle: "Where the Scriptures speak, we speak; and where the Scriptures are silent, we are silent." It was not a new denomination that he planned, but a union of all Christians on this Biblical basis, without added tests of creed or ritual. In August, 1809, Thomas Campbell organized the Christian Association of Washington—so-called from the Pennsylvania county of its origin—and for it he prepared the "Declaration and Address" which has since been regarded as a fundamental document of what was to be known as the Disciples movement. The same year Thomas Campbell's son, Alexander (1788-1866), emigrated to America, and was soon to outstrip his father in fame as an advocate of the former's views.

# A Bold New Dream

## by

## Melvin E. Dieter

**PRESSED** by the rapidly changing patterns of life in their post-war (Civil War) communities and churches, many of the converts of the holiness revival turned to the incipient institutions of the movement to find identity and community. These holiness bands of associations shared in the sense of unity, which had become common among members of American evangelical churches who met and worked together in joint evangelism. Out of those experiences, revivalists had boldly spoken of a coming day when the revival would eventuate in one united church. In the restoration, they said, a true, spiritual brotherhood would subsume the differences among, what to them, were the obviously deficient denominations. The visible unity of the church would be restored.

The rhetoric of the holiness partisans concerning the unity which the general acceptance of the holiness experience would bring among the churches was stronger than the rhetoric on Christian unity in any other segment of the American revival. Faced with the opposition of their own churches, which, they felt, were progressively falling away from the puritan-pietism life-style, which the holiness advocates commonly recognized as an integral part of genuine Christian witness, they applied the combined teleology of the logic of their message of perfectionism and their doctrines of present purification by the Holy Spirit to the questions of their church relations and the nature of the church itself.

That logical union, reinforced by the vitality of the idealistic dreams represented by the expansive mood of America's belief in her manifest destiny, resulted in a challenge to the holiness movement and the American "sects" to fulfill the revival's promise of a pure, unified, visible church. A small group of radical pioneers (including D. S. Warner) began to call for a radical reformation of the churches. In the real perfection in love which they believed the Holy Spirit had made possible for every Christian now, they saw the potential for the restoration of the perfection of the primitive church of Pentecost, in which the "saints" and the "sanctified" would gather together once again in undivided Christian witness. The divine patterns of that church, they felt, had been obscured by the accumulation of human creeds and ecclesiasticism. Out of their own commitment to perfectionism, they proclaimed that God had revealed the mystery of the restoration of his true church; it was to be a church of God: pure and one, comprised of people who were freed from selfish partisanship by entire sanctification by faith. For them, the holiness revival was the testimony to this new "age of the Spirit."

It was a bold new dream, made even bolder by the growing negative reaction of the churches to the perfectionist's optimistic claims. There was little hope, therefore, that the denominations would accept the ultimate conclusions of the radical application of that perfectionism to their own structure. Moreover, most segments of the holiness movement, itself, were equally unprepared to accept the radical reformer's conclusions. They were genuinely dedicated to Methodism's own commitment to order and organization. Beginning with Methodism, though admittedly increasingly reluctant Methodism, they continued to hope to usher in the long anticipated reformation of the many churches into one great holiness crusade.

The rapid deterioration of relations between the movement and the churches within a decade after the separation of the radicals (e.g., the Church of God Reformation Movement) from the churches forced many moderates in the movement to take their own reluctant steps toward "come-outism." The process was almost identical with that which they had so roundly condemned previously. By 1900, they too, apparently felt that the holiness revival's aggressive zeal to usher in a new day of hope for the world, in the "age of the Spirit," could not survive among the established churches. In that measure, they were acknowledging that the radicals had been right; to survive in the future, they agreed the promotion of the dream had to be carried on in structures which were more congenial to its own character and ends.

# The Disciples' Heritage

## by

## Ruth Rouse and Stephen Neill

From *A History of the Ecumenical Movement, 1517-1948,* ed. by Ruth Rouse and Stephen C. Neill. Published in the United States by The Westminister Press, 1954; reprinted 1967. Copyright © by The Trustees of the Society for Promoting Christian Knowledge, 1953. Used by permission.

**AT THEIR BEST,** Disciples have thought of themselves as a movement within the Church seeking after the unity of the Church. While sometimes uncomfortably aware of tensions within their own body, they insist that their fundamental aim is still the same, namely to unite Christians and to make Christianity more effective and more universal by strengthening loyalty to Christ combined with liberty in theological opinions.

The questions of the originality of the message of the Campbells has been carefully worked out by Disciples historians. There was nothing particularly new in Campbell's plea to restore the apostolic ordinances, for that has been attempted in all Christian generations and by many denominations. The Glasites or Sandemanians and the Haldane brothers of Scotland also held the same principles, and their influence upon the Campbells is well known. What was new in the Campbells' teaching was their unitive motive, whereby they sought to promote the unity of the Church through the restoration of primitive Christianity. And this was new only as compared with the Scottish developments, for it was not unique in America.

At the time of the Second Awakening, when the Campbells were beginning their reforming labours, there appeared in isolated sections of the United States several movements parallel to the Disciples. These took the Bible alone for their creed, called themselves simply "Christians," and hoped on that basis to unite a divided American Protestantism. Elias Smith (1769-1840) of New England, James O'Kelly (1735-1826), the ex-Methodist circuit-rider who founded the Republican Methodist Church in Virginia and North Carolina, and Barton W. Stone (1772-1844) of Kentucky, all contributed "Christian" movements to the American denominational map. Some of these later merged with the Disciples of Campbell; others joined in 1931 with the Congregational Churches to form the Congregational Christian Churches; and still others remain separate as the "Churches of Christ." Even in the German-speaking areas of Pennsylvania there was a "Christian" movement, led by an ex-Reformed minister named John Winebrenner (1797-1870), who founded the "Church of God." Like the Campbells and these other "Christian" prophets, Winebrenner felt "it is contrary to scripture to divide the church of God into different sects and denominations."

It is one of the ironies of history that all these movements, starting on the premise of restoring the unity of a divided Christendom, crystallized into denominations.

# Rise of the General Eldership

### by

### Kenneth Scott Latourette

Excerpted from *Christianity in a Revolutionary Age,* Vol. III (New York: Harper and Row, Inc., Copyright © 1961). Used by permission.

# A Time to Remember: BEGINNINGS

**SLIGHTLY EARLIER** than the Church of Latter Day Saints, like it emerging from the revival movements in the fore part of the nineteenth century but keeping more closely to the tradition of the Evangelical-Pietist stream of Protestantism, was the General Eldership of the Churches of God in North America. It arose primarily in the German Reformed Church (later called the Reformed Church in the United States), and mainly among those of German descent in Pennsylvania, but it also spread into the Western states. Its founder was John Winebrenner (1797-1860). The son of a prosperous German farmer in Pennsylvania, he was reared in the Reformed Church and became a minister in that body. During his student days, at the age of twenty, he had a deep religious experience of the Pietist kind, and under his preaching revivals broke out. He felt impelled to leave the Reformed Church and to help nourish congregations of those who had been born again. Like those in the awakenings who adopted the simple name of Christian or Disciples of Christ, he wished to restore primitive Christianity. To this end he and his followers adopted for their congregations the designation "Church of God," because they found it repeatedly in the New Testament, and a presbyterian form of church government, for which they believed New Testament precedent also existed. In theology the Churches of God were Arminian rather than Calvinistic. They believed three ordinances to be commanded in the New Testament—the baptism of believers only and by immersion only, the Lord's Supper, and the washing of feet. The latter two were always observed together and in the evening. Through the evangelistic preaching of Winebrenner and his co-labourers the Churches of God multiplied, especially in Maryland and Pennsylvania and then in the Middle West.

In the 1870s a division occurred in the General Eldership of the Churches of God. It was led by D. S. Warner, who was expelled from that body for what it deemed heretical views. He taught entire sanctification as a second work of grace, divine healing, and extreme asceticism. Those who followed him rejected all creeds, recognized "the Lord's people" in all denominations, and sought to bring about the identity, or at least the possible identity, of the visible and the invisible church. The Churches of God which arose from Warner's movement had their headquarters at Anderson, Indiana, and this was generally used to differentiate them from the others bearing that name.

# Vision of John Winebrenner

### by

### Richard Kern

Excerpted from *John Winebrenner, Nineteenth Century Reformer* (Harrisburg, Pa.: Central Publishing House, Copyright © 1974). Used by permission of the author.

**WINEBRENNER** himself telescoped the story of events in 1825 and after as follows:

> About this time (1825) more extensive and glorious revivals of religion commenced in different towns and neighbourhoods, to wit: New Cumberland, Linglestown, Middletown, Millerstown, Lebanon, Lancaster, Shippensburg, Elizabethtown, Mount Joy, Marietta, and various other places. In these glorious revivals there were hundreds and multitudes happily converted to God. The conversion of these scores and multitudes in different places led to the organization of churches. And, as the writer's views had by this time materially changed, as to the true nature of a scriptural organization of churches, he adopted the apostolic plan as taught in the New Testament, and established spiritual, free, and independent churches, consisting of believers or Christians only, without any human name, or creed, or ordinances, or laws, etc.

For Winebrenner then, the underlying or motivating principle in the establishment of these independent churches soon came to be thought of as the restoration of primitive or Biblical Christianity, i.e., what Winebrenner and his followers conceived of as being ''the apostolic plan, as taught in the New Testament''; hence, eventually, the concept of the local ''church of God.''

The church, Winebrenner reasoned, is a Biblical institution (although Winebrenner confined its origins to the New Testament). It therefore should have a Biblical name, *viz*. ''Church of God,'' and not a human one. Winebrenner explained:

> The name or title, Church of God, is undeniably the true and proper appellation by which the New Testament church ought to be designated. This is her scriptural and appropriate name. This, and no other title, is given her by divine authority. This name or title, therefore, ought to be adopted and worn to the exclusion of all others.
>
> There are those, who have pleaded for the use, and for the exclusive use, of some other appellations: such as the name of Christian; others for that of Disciples; and others, again, for the name Brethren, etc. But it ought to be recollected, that not one of those is a proper noun, or a patronymic, and, therefore, none of them is ever used in Scripture as an appellation for the church. The individual members of the church are, and may be, very properly so called; but not so with regard to the church herself. We nowhere read of the ''Christian Church,'' or of the ''Disciples' Church,'' nor of the ''Brethren's Church,'' etc.

This emphasis on a biblical name and scriptural foundation for the church enabled Winebrenner and his friends to argue against the charge that the "Church of God" or "churches of God" was the beginning of a new denomination. The "Church of God" was merely the "re-emergence," as it were, of the apostolic church and hence should be considered *The* Church rather than *a* church. To be sure, there were Christians, or "converted persons," in church organizations other than the churches of God, but only in the churches of God had Christians re-discovered or restored the apostolic plan of the church. Hence, the "Church of God" so conceived was a reform, and, to some extent, unity movement within the American church as a whole.

# The Need of the Times

### by

### John W. V. Smith

Excerpted from *Truth Marches On* (Anderson, Ind.: Gospel Trumpet Company, Copyright © 1956).

**THE FIRST** observation about this movement is that from the very beginning it was closely related to the life and times of the people. It was a true reformation in that it sought to bring about actual changes in church conditions and practices. The foundations of this reformation were fashioned in the crucible of real life. They did not grow out of a new philosophy nor even out of a new interpretation of Christian theology. The chief concerns of the early leaders and those who joined with them were the close-to-life matters of midwestern America in the late nineteenth century. A look at these conditions is necessary if one is to have a proper understanding of the developments which took place.

The period following the American Civil War saw marked changes in religious attitudes and interests. Both the thinking and the practice of Christian churches were in a process of transition. In the older churches along the Atlantic seaboard a strong reaction against the revivalism of an earlier time had developed and was accompanied by more than a slight tendency toward a new liberalism in theology, with many basic beliefs being called into question. The low moral tone of society in general brought a wave of religious indifference, and the spirit of secularism had come to dominate many of the clergy and their congregations. Practically all churches were much less insistent than formerly on a definite religious experience as a qualification for membership, with the result that the line between the "saved" and the "unsaved" became less and less distinct. In general, the witness of the churches was not a vital one. People were more interested in discussing Darwin's *On the Origin of Species* than in obtaining salvation for their souls.

In the Middle West these same tendencies were also in evidence, despite the postwar efforts of some of the churches to conduct revivals. In the main it may be said that the dying embers of evangelistic zeal were divided among the various denominations and were used to start new fires of loyalty to the separate groups. This resurgent sectarianism resulted in a sharper drawing of the lines which separated Christians from each other, and bitter rivalry arose among the several competing denominations. Schism broke the ranks of some of the larger communions and a number of new competitors entered the field through this splintering process. This was indeed the heyday of militant sectarianism.

The total impact of all this competitive activity did not bring any life to American Christianity, however. With certain notable exceptions it may be said that the churches of this period had a shortened view of their mission and a distorted sense of direction. The Great Commission was usually defined in terms of making additions to the membership rolls—often at the expense of other groups who were trying to do the same. Obviously this was a goal far short of the New Testament challenge to preach the gospel of love and repentance. In the main it may be said that the American Christianity of this time was shallow and was moving in the direction of disunity and competition rather than toward unity and cooperation.

One cooperative venture, however, transcended the barriers of denominationalism and sought to remedy some of the existing evils. This was the holiness movement. Although a loosely organized enterprise, its efforts never completely coordinated, the National Association for the Promotion of Holiness, first organized in Vineland, New Jersey, in July of 1867, was a concrete expression of a rather widespread desire to restore genuine Christian piety. Through sponsoring holiness camp meetings and encouraging the distribution of holiness literature this organization sought to promote the preaching of experiential religion, particularly the doctrine of sanctification, among the various ministers who were receptive to this kind of emphasis. The leaders were very careful, however, to do no violence to the denominational system. In most instances membership in a denomination was necessary in order to be a member of the Association. Thus, the believers in holiness were given opportunity to stand against the wickedness and shallow religion of the day, but in so doing they were forced to defend the disunity of the church and the competitive character of its witness.

D. S. Warner and many of the other early leaders of the Church of God reformation were associated with the holiness movement. They were attracted by the positive emphasis on personal piety which they found among these brethren. They were free to appropriate the truths which had been lifted up by the holiness people, but they were not satisfied to let the unhealthy condition of the church itself go unchallenged. In a most straightforward manner they came to grips with this issue and pointed an accusing finger at the sinful divisions in the body of Christ. These bold men issued a call to sincere Christians everywhere to sever their relations with "sectism" and to stand in the truth of God alone. They had no finespun theological theories to promote, but they were greatly concerned about the tragically divided state of the church. They sought to restore its unity and holiness in the most direct way possible.

It thus becomes apparent that the Church of God reformation was born out of a deep sensitivity to the acute needs of Christianity as it existed at this particular time and place in history. The movement is to be understood and its genius is to be explained only as this life-situation context is recognized. Any later tendencies in the group to be aloof from the grass-roots problems of the Christian world or any inclinations to define its mission in purely theoretical terms are strictly departures from the original character of the movement. The early leaders were not ivory-tower dreamers. They were close to the needs of their world, and their strategy for meeting those needs was direct action.

RIVER MINISTRY. The Church of God reached many people along the Ohio River in the 1890s with the "Floating Bethel," a flatboat that G. T. Clayton and his helpers outfitted as a church on the water. D. S. Warner, H. M. Riggle, A. T. Rowe, and several other ministers worked on the "Bethel."

BOOM TOWN. Typical of the radical changes that America experienced in the late 1800s was Anderson, Ind., which grew rapidly after natural gas was discovered there in 1887. The Gospel Trumpet Company moved to Anderson in 1906.

GOSPEL QUARTET. This group of gospel singers traveled all across North America in 1886-1890. From left to right: Barney E. Warren, D. S. Warner, Nannie Kigar, "Mother" Sarah Smith, and Frankie Miller.

BAPTISMAL SERVICE. The early evangelists had to "make do" with whatever situation they found. Here a Church of God minister baptizes new converts in the river at Neosho Falls, Kan., sometime in the 1890s.

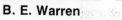
B. E. Warren

G. T. Office in Moundsville

A quilting bee to raise money for missions

An early Sunday school in Springfield, Ohio

**Breaking ground for G. T. office in Anderson, 1910**

**Gospel Trumpet Company office scene, 1913**

The Gospel Trumpet introduced
many people to the Church of God

Old Auditorium on Anderson campgrounds, about 1915

Wooden tabernacle in Anderson, early 1940s

Warner Auditorium in Anderson, 1977

# A Date with Destiny

### by

### Charles E. Brown

Excerpted from *When the Trumpet Sounded* (Anderson, Ind.: The Warner Press, Copyright © 1951).

**THE YEAR 1842** has been called "the year of decision." Undoubtedly it was one of those turns of the road for the American nation. The western boundary of the United States lay just west of what is now the state of Louisiana, and wound uncertainly north and west to a point a little south and west of Pike's Peak, Colorado, and then northward to a point a little north of Great Salt Lake, and then westward to the Pacific Ocean. The Oregon Territory, containing what are now the states of Oregon and Washington, was held jointly by the United States and Great Britain.

Mention is made of this vast stretch of American soil, not yet United States territory, to suggest the changes that have come over our country since 1842 and also to indicate how the national stage was set for a crisis just at this time. For instance, the Mormons were still at Nauvoo, Illinois, on the Mississippi River, ready to start in a few years on their great trek to a district which is now within the state of Utah, but was at that time under the authority of the Republic of Mexico. What is now Texas was then an independent state—the Republic of Texas. A little later it was to become a state of the Union. Meanwhile in the year 1842 war with Mexico was brewing over these matters.

# A Time to Remember: BEGINNINGS

The America of 1842 was a strange mixture of the past and the future. The cabins of the immigrants, stretching for hundreds of miles across the country from western Pennsylvania to the Mississippi River, were as crude as the huts of medieval peasants in Europe, and yet cities were springing to life across the land. Full of assorted miseries and crowded with immigrants from Europe, they were beginning to flower with the wealth of the industrial age. Railroads were reaching out weak and timid fingers from the East, but throughout the Middle West the covered wagons of the immigrants, massed in long trains that stretched to the Pacific Coast, were the principal means of travel.

The great revival which had lasted for some fifty years was gradually slowing down. Many thought that the tremendous excitement of the Millerite delusion tended to retard the real revival. William Miller, a Baptist preacher, had predicted the coming of Christ in 1843. Later he made it more definite—October 24, 1844. At the time of which we write religious circles were seething with excitement. Miller's followers numbered into the thousands, and on the set day they assembled in white robes to greet their Lord.

This was also the beginning of a great age in industry. John D. Rockefeller was a little boy three years old, and Thomas A. Edison would come along about five years later. Out in southern Indiana Abraham Lincoln was a sober-faced lad of twelve, preparing for his great task.

This was the world into which Daniel Sidney Warner was born on June 25, 1842, into the home of a tavern keeper at Bristol (now Marshallville), Ohio.

# Warner's Heresy: Holiness

### by

### Charles E. Brown

Excerpted from *When the Trumpet Sounded* (Anderson, Ind.: The Warner Press, Copyright © 1951).

**D. S. WARNER** loved the Winebrennerian communion. At first it conformed almost completely to his conception of the apostolic church. At the beginning of his ministry he had sacrificed all hopes of popularity and prestige by giving his allegiance to that small and insignificant group who endured much popular contempt because of their narrow, sectarian habits of life. In that part of Ohio they were called the "Johnny-cake church." Now Warner was to experience one of the bitterest disappointments of life to have this small group, for whom he had sacrificed so much, turn upon him and rend him with hostility, only because he had taken a further step on that road of sheer idealism which had brought him to them in the first place.

The whole story is long and dispiriting. It is the story of the reformers all over again—Luther cursed by the pope; George Fox and John Bunyan jailed by the church; Wesley hounded by his fellow Anglican priests. The record is played over and over again in the sempiternal funeral music of the church's pain and suffering. But always out of all its song of sorrow there arise the clear notes of spiritual victory.

Warner thought he could preach holiness among these people whom he loved so well and finally induce its acceptance by them. His disillusionment was a shocking experience, for which he had not long to wait.

After experiencing entire sanctification he threw himself into the work of the Holiness Movement with enthusiasm while still attending to his circuit. But the combination did not work well, from the standpoint of expediency. On September 15, 1877, a fellow elder, W. H. Oliver, presented to him charges to be preferred against him before the coming meeting of the Eldership. When these charges were presented against Warner at the Smithville, Ohio, meeting of the Eldership on September 27, 1877, Warner found himself charged with "inviting a set of fanatics calling themselves the Holy Alliance Band to hold meetings in the local Churches of God without consulting the elders or trustees or myself . . . joining in with these said bands and bidding them Godspeed and thereby bringing schism and division among these churches. . . . For the accommodation of this professed holy band that he invited to hold a meeting of ten days in the Church of God Chapel in Mansfield, Elder D. S. Warner did on the evening of the eighth of July in less than one hour hold the ordinances of washing the saints' feet and the Lord's Supper attended to . . . stating publicly in Shenandoah about the twenty-sixth of August that he had been preaching his own doctrine prior to seeking . . . holiness."

When the trial got into full swing somebody added the charge of "insanity whenever I touched on sanctification, also with causing division and schism in the churches and every evil work imaginable."

Warner boldly professed the experience and defended the doctrine of entire sanctification, and candor compels the admission that the brethren were, from their standpoint, charitable toward him. The committee reported "charges sustained," but recommended him favorably to the body for license with this restriction only, that he should not bring holiness workers or any outside elements to hold a meeting anywhere in the Churches of God without their consent. Warner says, "This I readily consented to as a meeting thus appointed could do no good, or but little." Warner's license was then renewed and he was appointed to a circuit at Canton, Ohio.

Here there is a pitiful story of searching for a cheap dwelling house in the poor part of the town, and then a long search, driving sixteen miles in an open buggy through the mud and cold, looking for wood and hay. The town did not even have a house of worship for his group and their meetings were held in the homes of the members.

Suddenly on November 23 he received a call from the Lord to

resign this circuit and give himself to holiness evangelism. This he proceeded to do, and on December 19 he removed from Canton to Upper Sandusky to the home of his wife's parents. It was not long until he was active in holiness evangelism. An indication of his industry and zeal in the work is given by an entry in his journal for January 26, 1878, when he and Brother Linsey stayed up all night in prayer to God for Findlay, Ohio: "God rolled upon our hearts a dreadful agony for souls and gave us an awful sight of the wicked apostasy of the churches." The results of his ministry here were as they were to be for many years to come—a wonderful record of souls saved and sanctified and of the sick healed. But along with that came strong opposition and very soon a threat of further prosecution before the ecclesiastical courts. No time was lost in fulfilling this threat. Already on October 1, 1877, the General Eldership had sustained charges against him for preaching holiness, but had condoned his alleged offense and issued him a restricted license. Now only four months later, on January 30, 1878, the standing committee again heard charges against him for (1) transcending the restrictions of the Eldership, (2) violating rules of co-operation, (3) participating in dividing the church. It seems a waste of time to go into these charges and the defense concerning them. From the standpoint of the present writer the trial of a minister for preaching holiness can never be anything but a farce, and conviction of such a charge is the highest honor a true minister of the gospel could ever hope to have. Warner showed that "the only results of the holiness meeting were 53 sinners converted and 118 believers sanctified."

The next day after the trial Warner met one of the committee on a train and was not even enough interested to ask him what decision the standing committee had reached. Eventually the committeeman broke the news that the standing committee had sustained the charges against Warner and had withheld his license.

Dr. Forney, in his *History of the Churches of God*, says:

> During several of these years the Eldership was
> contending against the inroads of heresies

advocated by D. S. Warner. It had finally to resort to the old remedy of excision in order to prevent the spread of the disease and restore the body to good health.

The denomination did not stop with curing the ''disease of holiness'' by the surgical removal of Warner; it also set up quarantines against this doctrine. Dr. Forney says of the Eldership meeting the following September:

> The Warner case was indirectly revived when the committee on resolutions adopted the following: That any minister of this body that may presume to preach the dogma of a second work for sanctification shall be deemed unsound in the theology of the Church of God and should not hold an ecclesiastical relation as a minister in this Eldership.

As a piece of ecclesiastical surgery, the excision of Warner was a skillful operation. However, the patient did not die and the work which Warner represented outgrew the organization from which he was expelled in numbers and in success within a generation.

Warner was now free and he continued to engage in holiness evangelistic work with great zeal and success. He preached in Findlay, Upper Sandusky, Dunkirk, Tiffin, and Mansfield, in north central Ohio. On March 7, 1878, he tried organizing a new church. In his journal he writes as follows under that date:

> Wrote evening. Upper Sandusky. John 3:19. Fellowshiped some fourteen souls in the Church of God, formed on a congregational basis and with holiness the principal foundation stone. On the 31st of last January the Lord showed me that holiness could never prosper upon sectarian soil, encumbered by human creeds, and party names, and he gave me a new commission to

join holiness and all truth together and build up
the apostolical church of the living God. Praise
his name, I will obey him!

Evidently Warner was feeling his way toward a new
realization of the fellowship of the apostolic church of the New
Testament. This particular experiment was never repeated, so
far as we know, and it represents a very definite step toward that
clear conviction he finally reached.

# A Reluctant Beginning

## by

## John W. V. Smith

Excerpted from *Truth Marches On* (Anderson, Ind.: Gospel
Trumpet Company, Copyright © 1956).

**ALMOST FOUR** years elapsed between the time (January,
1878) when Warner first received his "new commission to join
holiness and all truth together," and those dramatic events at
Beaver Dam, Indiana, and Carson City, Michigan, in October
of 1881. These certainly were not drastic spur-of-the-moment
actions without careful consideration of all the implications
involved. It was also in 1878 that another of the early leaders,
A. J. Kilpatrick, first began to "see the light." In leaving the
United Brethren church he declared, "Every person who has
salvation and belongs to a denominational church belongs to
two, and Jesus built only one church and said that the gates of
hell should not prevail against it." Warner and Kilpatrick met in
Payne, Ohio, in 1879 and discovered that their views were
almost identical. It is reported that at this meeting each man
renounced his sectarian ordination to the ministry and then each
in turn ordained the other. This was a perfect setting for
announcing the launching of a new movement, but no such

announcement was made. Warner also had conversations with various others, such as J. C. Fisher and his wife, Allie, Jeremiah Cole, and W. J. Henry, but none of these contacts resulted in any premature action.

Part of the reason for this delay in getting started was undoubtedly the lack of any clear direction concerning the proper action to take. They did not want to be accused of starting another sect, and they were reluctant to disrupt what little harmony there was within and among the various churches. As time went on, though, they became convinced that unity within the framework of the sectarian system was an impossibility. Furthermore, they were certain that the time had arrived when God was calling his people out of this sinful system. So they took the bold step and declared themselves free from all man-made sects and members only of the one holy church of God. Once this definite break had been made there was no longer any hesitancy to speak or to act. Fearlessly they declared their position wherever they could find an audience, and without apology they called upon all true Christians to abandon the sects in which they were scattered so they might participate in the pure fellowship of the redeemed without restrictions.

# We Forever Withdraw!

### by

### Daniel S. Warner

Excerpted from *Birth of a Reformation,* by Andrew L. Byers. (Anderson, Ind.: Gospel Trumpet Company, Copyright © 1921). Reprinted by Faith Publishing House, Guthrie, Okla.

**DANIEL S. WARNER'S** account of how he was led to sever his connection with the holiness association, which he began to see was but a milder form of sectism, is given in an editorial for June 1, 1881:

> Saturday, April 22, the hand of the Lord was heavily upon our soul, had no relish to converse with any one but God. Finally in company with two brethren we went into the house of God at Hardinsburg, Ind., and placed ourselves under the searching eye of God, when the Spirit of the Lord showed me the inconsistency of repudiating sects and yet belonging to an association that is based upon sect recognition. We promised God to withdraw from all such compacts. But being dearly attached to the holiness work, we attended the Association at Terre Haute, and tried to have the sect-endorsing clause removed from the constitution. Its substance is as follows, speaking of local associations:
>
> "It shall consist of members of various Christian organizations and seek to work in harmony with all these societies."
>
> We offered the following substitute: "It shall consist of, and seek to cooperate with, all true Christians everywhere."
>
> We had supposed that fellowship and cooperation should not exclude any person or truth that is in Christ Jesus, and that we should not be compelled to bow down to anything not in, nor of, Christ Jesus.
>
> We were positively denied membership on the ground of not adhering to any sect. And now we wish to announce to all that we wish to cooperate with all Christians, as such, in saving souls—but **forever withdraw** from all organisms that uphold and endorse sects and denominations in the body of Christ.

# Keeping out of Babylon

## by

### Andrew L. Byers

Excerpted from *Birth of a Reformation* (Anderson, Ind.: Gospel Trumpet Company, Copyright © 1921). Reprinted by Faith Publishing House, Guthrie, Okla.

**AN EVENT** that had to occur sooner or later was Brother Warner's separation from the Northern Indiana Eldership. At the Eldership meeting which convened at Beaver Dam, Kosciusko County, Ind., in October, 1881, he proposed some measures by which that body might be made to conform more perfectly to the Bible standard with reference to government. In this he would not be heard, and on their rejection of his reform measures he realized, probably for the first time, that the new Eldership, bent on continuing their human organization, was a sect with which he must sever his connection, and he then and there did so. This event does not properly mark his coming out of spiritual Babylon, as some have supposed. In heart he had already been out, and had preached against sects. But he ignorantly supposed that the Northern Indiana Eldership of the Church of God was not a sect and therefore that he was keeping clear of sects. Thus his act at Beaver Dam was a *keeping* out of Babylon as much as a coming out. It was the latter only in the outward sense, but of course it emphasized and gave more definite character to the anti-sectarian stand he had previously taken.

There were others in attendance at the Eldership meeting who had heard his preaching against spiritual Babylon and who also took the same step with him. They were David Leininger, William Ballenger and wife, and F. Krause and wife. We give their names as being of those originals who declared themselves free from all outward forms of Babylon.

A similar thing occurred in Michigan. About the same time the Northern Indiana Eldership was formed, there originated near Pompeii, Gratiot County, Mich., the Northern Michigan

Eldership of the Church of God. This body was formed because its members had been isolated from and generally dissatisfied with the old Eldership, which sanctioned secrecy and was steeped in tobacco. About the fall of 1878 there joined this new Eldership J. C. Fisher and his wife, Allie R. They had never heard of Brother Warner at that time. In the spring of 1880, J. C. Fisher had occasion to visit Indiana on business, and it happened that while there he heard Brother Warner preach, and he accepted the doctrine of holiness and received the experience. The following autumn the Fishers sent for Brother Warner to come up to that part of Michigan and preach holiness. It was then that Allie R. consecrated for and also received the experience of sanctification.

A year later, just before the annual meeting of the Eldership (October, 1881), the Fishers and others, thinking to get the Eldership to accept holiness and thus make good the claim of being the true church, started a holiness meeting at Carson City, where the Fishers lived, and again had Brother Warner present. This was right after the meeting in Indiana where Brother Warner had declared his separation from the Northern Indiana Eldership. The situation was similar to what it had been in Indiana. Brother Warner had been preaching on the true church and setting forth its divine government, and the hope of these Michigan saints was that if they could get the Eldership to accept holiness they might get them to do away with the human machinery and fill the true church requirement. In this they were disappointed. Before the holiness meeting was over the Eldership showed its opposition. Upon this the Fishers and a good number of others, nearly twenty in all, withdrew from the Eldership.

Thus there were two centers where a stand of independence with regard to the Eldership and human ecclesiasticism had been taken. These two congregations of saints—at Beaver Dam, (Ind.), and Carson City, (Mich.),—were the earliest in the United States (so far as the author knows) who had stepped completely out of Babylon and had taken for their basis that of the New Testament church alone. An annual camp-meeting was established at each place.

# A New Epoch for the Church

by

**Andrew L. Byers**

Excerpted from *Birth of a Reformation* (Anderson, Ind.: Gospel Trumpet Company, Copyright © 1921). Reprinted by Faith Publishing House, Guthrie, Okla.

**LOOKING BACK** upon Brother Warner's career it would seem that his connection with the Church of God (Winebrennerian), which assumed to have no creed but the Bible and to be indeed the true church of God, had doubtless served to emphasize to him the true church ideal and to shape his course along right lines. And his rejection by the Ohio Eldership for the preaching of holiness awakened him to see that that body was not what it claimed to be, but was, after all, only a humanly ruled institution, only one sect among the many. The light he already had on the church was sufficient to forbid his reuniting with them. Thus the so-called Church of God had contributed to him the right idea of the church, and the holiness movement had brought to his understanding the line on which God would bring out a pure church, namely, the line of holiness; and thus was the divine Hand leading him and fitting him for the work to which he was called.

We can only imagine what it meant to step out on God alone and preach the divine judgments against the apostate religions of the day, to decry the evils of denominationalism, and to undertake on that same line the publication of a paper. That his work was despised and that Satan undertook to crush it in its very beginning can not be wondered at. Its humbleness and apparent insignificance looked uninviting to the worldly-minded; but the deep spirituality and divine manifestations that characterized it were a sufficient vindication to those who were capable of spiritually discerning the truth. There was something that said, "This work is of God." There was a sense of spiritual freedom and of love and Christian fellowship that bore convincing testimony to those who would but listen to the dictation of the Spirit that this is indeed the truth.

But Brother Warner was not alone. God had reserved his thousands who no longer were bowing the knee to Baal. From them he received encouragement and support, though for a few years it seemed his work had to go through the crucible of trial. Accordingly we trace his difficulties and sorrows, as well as his victories, until the cause becomes fully established in the earth.

From what we learn of Brother Warner's earlier views and attitude, he never had a party spirit; he never was a sectarian. Even from his early ministry the love and fellowship that exists among the people of God he recognized as the paramount bond of Christian union. After his conversion, when dealing with the question of what church he should join, he is found casting about to determine which one represented the real church of God. As the followers of Winebrenner had the right name, and seemed to him to be correct in doctrine, he was led into that denomination. With the insufficient light he then possessed he probably failed to see the man rule that prevailed, instead of the Holy Spirit rule that characterizes the divine, theocratic government in the true church of God. He discovered, of course, the clash of this man rule with the free, independent inclination of the Holy Spirit, by which he preferred to be led. But he bore with it patiently, believing that he was in the true church; and it took years for him to discover that the body to which he belonged was but a sect.

It was through the attainment of the Bible standard of holiness that he was gradually led into the truth respecting the church and sects. Early in 1878 he wrote: "The Lord showed me that holiness could never prosper upon sectarian soil encumbered by human creeds and party names, and he gave me a new commission to join holiness and all truth together and build up the apostolic church of the living God." He soon began to receive light on the Scriptures, which revealed to him that the church was to be restored to her primitive glory in the evening of the dispensation. The chapter on a Spiritual Shaking, taken from his book [*Bible Proofs of a Second Work of Grace*], clearly shows that when the chapter was written (1879) he understood that God was going to bring out a pure church. He published this in 1880, which became the date from which the present epoch of the church may be reckoned.

# The Origins of the Movement

## by

## Andrew L. Byers

Excerpted from *The Gospel Trumpet Publishing Work Described and Illustrated* (Anderson, Ind.: Gospel Trumpet Company, 1907).

**WE ARE** sometimes asked when, where, and through whom this movement originated. As has been said, the light is not new light, but light that was possessed by the early Christians, and that has been regained since the apostasy. It is simply the word of God itself taught, believed, practised, lived. The question, then, of "when, where, and through whom" loses itself in the word of God. There can be no religious reformation whose principles of truth were not already embodied in the word of truth itself.

Viewed as a reform movement, this work had its beginning in the holiness agitation.

As to *where* it began, it may be answered, In all places where there were the true spiritual people of God. In reply to *through whom*, the answer is, Not through any one person, but through the spiritual people in general and universally. As to *when* this movement began, the reader is directed back to about the seventies of the last century, to a great holiness agitation in many of the various denominations. It was from God and was the ushering in of a dispensation of judgment upon the apostate religions of the day. Those who were "at ease in Zion" began to realize a disturbance of their carnal security. It was the beginning of a great day of decision, when the corruption of men's hearts was to be so revealed that they could not endure the burning truth, but were compelled either to accept and walk in the light, or take their stand against the same and in many cases become filled with a double portion of carnal wickedness, even to the extent of displaying the manifestations of demons.

A great crisis had come, which should result in the gathering of God's people out of the various places where they had been scattered and held captive by the creeds of men. The spiritual people everywhere began to discern the fact that the corrupt sectarian denominations were not the church of God, and their hearts were being prepared for the angel's call, ''Come out of her, my people, that ye be not partakers of her sins, and that ye receive not of her plagues'' (Rev. 18:4).

Thus we comprehend the beginning of this reform movement. Thousands have left the bondage of spiritual Babylon to abide in the liberty there is in Christ alone and to enjoy the sweet fellowship and unity of the people of God who are free from all creeds and divisions. Perfected holiness in the heart leaves no room for sectarian elements. Entire sanctification makes God's people one, in accordance with the prayer of our Savior in behalf of his disciples: ''Sanctify them through thy truth . . . that they all may be one.''

That the Protestant sects, as well as Roman Catholicism, are a part of spiritual Babylon, is acknowledged by the best commentators and is no question in the minds of all godly people.

The deliverance of God's people became the real theme and object of the holiness reformation. Satan, anticipating this, devised many counterfeit movements. No longer able to deceive God's people by sectarian teaching, he attempted, by counterfeit, to falsify the doctrines of truth that are especially effective in establishing the true work of God.

A kind of sectarian holiness arose. In many instances of God's people leaving the Protestant denominations the sectarian ministers immediately began to preach holiness, thinking to retain those who were leaving. It is evident, of course, that sectarian holiness is not the genuine, for the latter is certainly destructive of sectarian elements. Holiness associations were formed in which the members could still retain membership in their respective denominations. False holiness became more plentiful than the true. The idea of leaving the churches (so called) began to be strongly denounced by many who had themselves accepted holiness.

The leaving of the sectarian denominations was counterfeited. Many came out of the sects who were false representatives of the truth, some opposing sanctification as a work of grace subsequent to justification, others opposing water baptism and the other New Testament ordinances—some clustering around one antichrist doctrine and some around another. The whole began to appear as a disgusting spectacle, and "come-outism," as it was odiously called, bore no convincing testimony of the truth of God. In this manner thousands have been and are still deceived.

Divine healing, which is one of the privileges extended in the gospel, was also counterfeited. "Divine healers" arose in various places, and through these Satan, who is ever ready to withdraw his afflicting hand provided he can impose some deception on the individual, has diverted many from the right way.

The fact that there are so many counterfeit movements only proves that there is a genuine. There is something about the real that the counterfeit never possesses. There were those in whom existed the real spirit of truth, whose teaching had the right ring, and whom God honored with the anointing of power and glory in the salvation of souls, both by word of mouth and by medium of the pen. The various associations and bodies that had arisen and that failed to represent the real reform movement also had their respective periodicals. But there was one that was willing to proclaim the whole truth without compromise.

It was no more than might be expected that a paper publishing the genuine messages of truth, making war on all religion that does not come up to the Bible standard, should bring upon itself a continued siege by all the hosts of Satan's kingdom in their efforts to crush it out of existence. Accordingly, were we to trace in detail the progress of the *Gospel Trumpet* publishing work we should note a constant struggle against the opposing forces of the enemy. Satan, Herodlike, endeavored to crush it in its very infancy, but God extended his protecting hand in its behalf, until today it stands as a mighty instrument for the dissemination of the present truth.

Truth always prevails over its foes, though it is never popular with the masses. This work is of God. Man's responsibility consists in humble submission to God, being fully consecrated to his service. "I have commanded my sanctified ones, I have also called my mighty ones for mine anger, even them that rejoice in my highness" (Isa. 13:3). Amen. Every one that is wholly sanctified is chosen to take a part in the work of this glorious and last reformation.

# Beginning of the Present Reformation

### by

### Robert L. Berry

Excerpted from *Golden Jubilee Book* (Anderson, Ind.: Gospel Trumpet Company, 1931).

**THE REFORMATION** of which we now speak is more complete and fundamental than any reformation preceding it. It ranges over so vast a territory that many, even of its most devoted advocates, have not comprehended its breadth.

The roots of the present reformation reach far back. Historically it is closely connected with the Wesleyan teaching on sanctification. During the time of Wesley, and later, holiness bands were organized here and there over the country, the members of which were deeply concerned with having perfect love and pure hearts. They were searchers after truth. They sought for the finest and best outward expression of divine grace in their lives and for the deepest infillings of the Spirit of God in their hearts.

All this is good parentage. The doctrine of entire sanctification as a definite second work of divine grace wrought in the heart after regeneration, as taught by Wesley, was a truth as solid as Gibraltar. The waves of criticism and opposition have never shaken the soundness of this teaching, and that heart appeal for more of. God, together with the teaching, was preparing hearts to receive a clearer revelation of divine truth.

God always prepares the way for what he intends to do. Before the Reformation of Luther's day he brought in the Renaissance and inspired the invention of printing. Before the present reformation God brought in the true Bible doctrine of holiness and sanctification and inspired holy men and women to seek his face for deeper grace.

It came like the early church came, and it was and is carried on by men free from the enslaving dogmas of narrow religions. It runs not in human channels cut out by human hands but it spreads over the broad expanse of spiritual truth joyously, bent on knowing all the will of God.

The greatness of the step taken by the pioneers of this movement may be partly envisioned when one remembers the complexion of Christianity in the middle of the nineteenth century. The church was divided into many sects. No one was thought to be a Christian unless he belonged to a denomination. There was much sectarian rivalry. The doctrines of the different churches were attacked with vigor. People were partisanly strong in their beliefs.

But in 1880 Daniel S. Warner and others severed their connection with humanly organized churches and boldly maintained that Christ had built a church and that membership in it was the only essential thing to consider. And therefore he and his associates made no effort to organize a church along denominational lines, but made their appeal direct to the Scripture itself. They contended that spiritual fellowship with Christ and with one another and devotion to scriptural ideals and practices were all the bonds that Christians needed.

They went further than that. They contended, and scripturally they were right, that sectarianism is a sin, that division in the church is condemnable, and that those who are guilty of dividing the church are guilty in the sight of God of rending the sacred body of Christ. They taught that the church, being made up of all those who are partakers of Christ, is essentially a spiritual affair, that naturally, being such, no man can build it.

That was extremely radical preaching for that day. Really it is very radical preaching yet. Or perhaps it should be called liberal. That matters not. But the remarkable fact is that many opposed this teaching and the early pioneers suffered considerably for the truth which they were declaring.

There were other steps they took beyond that bold, brave scriptural one on what the church is. They swung clear away from dogmatic theology as promulgated by the schools and went direct to the Scriptures as the very fountain of truth. What it taught they were ready to believe and accept and practice. A new attitude toward the Scriptures sprang up—the humble, open-hearted, obedient attitude, well expressed by the prophet's words: "Speak, Lord; for thy servant heareth." The Holy Spirit was accepted as the actual ruler of the church and to this day these are the principles held to by the Church of God. Nowhere, by any minister who has this light, will anyone be asked to join the church. Nowhere is any known Christian excluded from fellowship, no matter what his connections may be.

Daniel S. Warner was the boldest, most radical, most liberal thinker on Bible lines since the days of the apostles. At one sweep he stepped clear out into the very glory and simplicity of early Christianity and he pointed out the only way to church unity.

And now, fifty years since the pioneers struck out in a new path, we celebrate the event. Yea, more than that. To celebrate the past is easy. To hold fast to truth is more difficult. To look into the future and to go forward with Christ and truth along these same lines is most difficult.

No sooner had Daniel S. Warner and others begun to preach as men had not preached for time out of mind than men saw in their message the grandest truths the mind of man is capable of conceiving. They saw a church built up by Christ, led and organized by the Holy Spirit, the names of whose members are in the Lamb's book of life, which takes the Scriptures as its only discipline, and fellowships every blood-bought soul everywhere. Here is real Christian unity.

Despised and rejected in church circles, these men preached more real Bible truth in one sermon than one would expect in months of the ordinary kind. They preached profound truths; and it created a furor wherever they went. Thousands received scriptural light. Many joyfully embraced the great truths they heard and spared neither pains nor money to spread the message everywhere. Men were called from the plow handles and from the workbench; women felt the call and left their homemaking to share a greater responsibility. A new outburst of song occurred, and soon several hundred new songs came out to enrich Christian hymnody. Camp meetings were held, congregations became established, and the work went on and goes on.

# Heaven to Earth

### by

### Russell McCracken

Transcribed from the soundtrack of "From Heaven to Earth," a film produced for the Church of God by the Jam Handy Organization, Detroit, Mich., 1955.

**BRIGHTER DAYS** were sweetly dawning. The glory of God's creation was everywhere to behold in the rolling wonder of the countryside. In the mind's eye, one could see gentle Galilee in the fertile stretches of the American prairies. Some eighteen hundred and eighty years has past since the Lord's coming to set his people free, and there were those with music in their souls who spread the glad tidings. Sometimes the sound of their singing would float out across the countryside, and people hearing it over the hills before they saw the wagons would imagine the angels were singing.

The Bible says that all in every place that call upon the name of Jesus Christ and unto the church of God are "called to be saints." To them that are sanctified in Christ Jesus there be grace unto them and peace. The singers proclaimed this gospel truth. They called one another and the congregations "saints." They believed saintly living was possible here on earth. With praise and everlasting joy in their hearts, they believed that they were returning to Zion over the highway of holiness.

Jesus came from heaven to earth, they believed, to save all the nations and all the people from the Babel of confusion and strife. They believed that the joy of life was getting back to the blessed old Bible for the gospel truth and then going forward, ever forward in the progress to glory. They believed that the oneness of heaven should be reflected in the oneness of God's Church in this world below and that God's Church, the true Bible Church, had no creed but the Scriptures, no government but that guided by the Holy Spirit, no division of God's people into parties or denominations. Unity, holiness, heaven were their songs and their sermons.

They were vigorous men and women, young, and filled with the energies of the apostles of old. The saints, the singers, they were called—the believers, the workers, the laborers in the Lord's vineyard, the brothers and sisters, and ministers and helpers. They traveled the highway of holiness for the love of God and the glory of God. They preached the oneness of God's Church in such earthy American places as Rising Sun and Ridgeville, Claypool, Keokuk, Merrimac Springs, Silver Lake, Sandy Lake, Beaver Dam, Prospect Chapel, Praise Chapel, Mount Pleasant. And those who listened to the preaching were as earthy and American as the places and the preachers. Rugged folks, sturdy congregations, rough pioneers hardened by long hours of digging a livelihood from the land, farmers.

There were those from place to place who gave the gospel workers a mean time. There were those who confounded the call to salvation. They didn't want the freedom from sin and sinning. They threatened with tar and feathers, threatened to ride the gospel workers out of town on a rail. There were many breathless escapes. They feared not to suffer with the Savior. And many a detractor, many an oppressor, was brought to the altar, converted to Christ and, thus, brought into the Church of the living God. Many have raised their voices in penitence and contrition.

"In the beginning was the Word and the Word was with God"—and this reformation movement of the Church of God was believed a fulfillment of the promise, revealed in Bible prophecy, that the people of God's Kingdom on earth shall at last come together in Christ. It was believed that, through this movement, God was bringing his people "out of all places where they have been scattered in the cloudy and dark day" of denominations,—and that he was restoring anew the Church of the days of the apostles. Then there was "one fold and one shepherd." Then there was divine rule. Then the Church was flexible, capable of expansion and of going forward in all truth and of adjusting itself to all needs and conditions. Christian work was God and man working together in freedom from ecclesiastical dogma and ambition.

Throughout the ages, of course, many Christians have felt the sense of need for the restoring of this Church of God. Many were tortured or destroyed as heretics. Other reformations in church history have brought out various truths in the progress upward to the scriptural level. Wyclif, Huss, Luther, the Wesley brothers, all were instruments of God in carrying the reforming forward. The doctrine of justification by faith, the doctrine of sanctification by faith, and the witness of the Holy Spirit were successive steps toward a final unity of the Church. All Christians could unite on the basis of the Scriptures alone if the human element in the work of God were subjected to the divine. The human element created the denominations, and this movement meant an end to such division of God's people.

Many have heard the trumpet sounding. Many have lifted up their eyes to the vision of service in God's work. One of them was Daniel S. Warner, one of the first preachers of the Church of God reformation movement. Behind the bearded face of this gentle but fearless man radiated the spirit of the Nazarene of long ago. He didn't believe himself the "leader" of the movement. He believed that Jesus the captain leads back to the blessed old Bible, back to the light of the Word. He believed that "Holiness unto the Lord" should be on the banners of this movement forever.

And so it came to pass that the gospel singers, the gospel workers, traveled up and down and across the land. Itinerant evangelists they were called. They traveled in spring wagons generally, though sometimes by train. They asked nothing for their labors either from God or man but the salvation of souls and the glory of God. They were moving constantly. Their congregations were few and far between. Thus, they became known as a "flying ministry," always on the go—"go," as the Lord has spoken, "make disciples."

The "church" of God means the "congregation" of God, not the church building. In the early years of the movement, there were few church buildings available to the congregations. So they came together in many different places. There were grove meetings within the arching cathedrals of trees and beside the fresh water streams. There were barn meetings. There were cottage meetings. There were children's meetings. There were schoolhouse meetings where grown-ups crowded into the same seats where they had learned their ABCs. There were courthouse meetings, sometimes on the courthouse steps where the town would turn out to hear the preaching. There were camp meetings.

The general assemblies are the nearest the movement has ever come to what is known as "church government." For there is no hierarchy here, no worldly titles. The Holy Spirit guides the assemblies and there is spiritual democracy for everyone. The proceedings are based on the foundation of scriptural truth. Wherever and whenever the meetings were held, tracts were distributed, Christian literature circulated to carry the movement's message far and wide. From the beginning, the evangelists of the "flying ministry" were teachers as well as preachers. The Christian truths they expounded were buttressed with the Bible. And the call to Christian brotherhood went out to all people in all nations.

# A Time to Remember: BEGINNINGS

One of the first means of forwarding this task was the *Gospel Trumpet*, a little paper with reports of work in the field. It served to keep the traveling gospel workers in touch with one another and to spread the reformation movement of the Church of God. When the work started in a new place, it was usually because somebody there in some way or other had come across a copy of the *Gospel Trumpet* or other literature from the Gospel Trumpet Company. And oh, that publishing company had small beginnings! Just a simple hand press at first. It was years before the movement could afford a power press with a wood-burning boiler. And the day the wire-stitching machine came was a great and good day around the Gospel Trumpet office. It meant the company could then bind its own small books and tracts. Another great and good day was the day the first typewriter came. It was second-hand. It typed all capital letters. But it was highly welcomed in the service of the Lord.

Workers at the publishing company came to be known as "the Gospel Trumpet family." They dedicated themselves to the Lord's service and lived with it. They shared and shared alike an existence frugal indeed by worldly standards, but immensely rich by those of the Spirit. The Gospel Trumpet Home became a kind of ministers' institute or workers' training school. There the young prepared themselves to go forth and preach the gospel. Go—make disciples! And there it was indeed "home" to the journeying evangelists and missionaries. There they would stop back with their reports for the paper, new tracts, and always new songs. And how the Gospel Trumpet family loved to try out a new song! They would gather around the organ and lift their voices in resounding dedication. One and all, they had enlisted in his service. They were willing to work for Jesus and it was truly wonderful work.

In the early days of the movement, the Gospel Trumpet office moved about much in the manner of the "flying ministry." Rome City, Indianapolis, Cardington, Bucyrus, Williamston, Grand Junction, Moundsville, Anderson. Anderson in Indiana finally became the home of the publishing company and the home of the movement. There, from the rolling prairie land, there would arise the plant to print the message in succeeding years. There from the blessed acres of another Galilee there would arise the living quarters of the Gospel Trumpet family that would one day become Anderson College and Theological Seminary. Anderson in Indiana, a place to train and teach and inspire and inspirit the workers and the missionaries, the ministers and all those going forth with God in whatever calling and whatever walk of life.

The pioneers of this movement did consecrate this Galilee, this green pasture as the "home" for the movement, a shelter for world travelers, a gathering place, but only as any place in God's creation could be a gathering place, a shelter. Go, make disciples—this commission points the way to the "home" that is the world and the continued growth of this movement. Anderson in Indiana was only a place among many, many places for the work to grow and to go forward, ever forward. The pioneers could know this as they could know the Church of God reformation movement is the coming out of God's people "to be saints." East, West, North, South—in North America, South America, Europe, Africa, Asia and the far islands of the Pacific—the highways of the world were all highways of holiness returning to Zion.

The song they sang when they gathered together in the early years of the movement still lights the way to go. Go make disciples in God's truth. Rejoicing in the Lord and in the Lord's work, the saints, the singers, the believers, the laborers in the Lord's vineyard, brothers and sisters, the ministers and helpers—all from humble walks of life, wholesome, gentle, and pure in heart, they carried the message of the true Bible Church into the tomorrow that became today.

In the tomorrow that became today, these little ones became the men and women who have carried the work forward, ever forward, with the *Gospel Trumpet* and other publications, with such church developments as the Missionary Board and World Service, Church Extension and Christian Education, the Woman's Missionary Society, the colleges and seminary, Christian Brotherhood Hour, and Youth Fellowship. These little ones became the pastors and congregations raising missionary homes and houses of worship as an offering of praise for the love of God, the glory of God and the sturdy, steady continuation of the movement.

Did they vision—these children of yesterday—the faster tempo, the greater growth, the tremendous opportunity of the tomorrow that became today? Indeed they did. Like the early pioneers of this movement, they welcomed each new device just as that first typewriter with all its capital letters was welcomed, every invention of man that could prove useful in the service of the Lord.

"In the beginning was the Word and the Word was with God"—and the beginning is ever-present. It is always the eternal. These children and their children's children can sing with past generations of the Church of God reformation movement that offering of praise that is joy everlasting, faith and peace for the pure in heart.

# A Company of Gospel Singers

### by

### Andrew L. Byers

Excerpted from *Birth of a Reformation* (Anderson, Ind.: Gospel Trumpet Company, Copyright © 1921). Reprinted by Faith Publishing House, Guthrie, Okla.

**BROTHER WARNER** felt that he needed, and that the Lord was going to provide, a company of singers to go with him in the evangelistic field. It was about this time [1886] that the company who should travel with him for more than five years began to be formed. It was at the Williamston assembly that summer that Brother Warner said to Nannie Kigar, of Payne, Ohio, and to Frances Miller, of Battle Creek, who attended the meeting, that he felt impressed they would form a part of his company to help in singing and other gospel work. Their voices were soprano and alto respectively. They, with a number of other saints, accompanied Brother Warner to the Beaver Dam assembly. On their way, as they changed cars at Ft. Wayne, they met and were joined by Sarah Smith, of Jerry City, Ohio. While they were at Beaver Dam the Lord added Sister Smith to the company. Her voice furnished a high tenor. She was an elderly lady and she was called the ''mother'' of the company.

In the latter part of January he with his company of singers and co-workers went to Deerfield, Randolph County, Ind., arriving on a Saturday evening. The next morning they attended a meeting where a nominal Christian preacher had the service. They sang some of the sweet songs of victory; but this so confounded the preacher that he could not find anything in his

Bible to preach, and after he had taken the pulpit he invited Brother Warner to preach. The latter preached a burning message. He had hoped for the use of the house, but it could be seen that the preacher intended to control the house that week, for he proposed that he and these people use it alternately. He was soon told that they were out on the blood and fire line, that they could not yoke up with the dead priests of Babel and would go elsewhere.

They went over into the edge of Jay County and began meetings in a United Brethren house called Prospect. Here the preaching created a furor among those who were joined to their sectarian institution and felt that it was in danger. It was like a thunderbolt in the community. The singing drew the crowds. The trustees became fearful. One of them went into the woods to pray to know what to do to get rid of these people who seemed to be taking things. The heavenly songs seemed to follow him. He felt he should attend all the meetings to see what occurred. He soon found that these people had something more than the United Brethren had. He was one of two trustees who embraced the truth, and of course desired that the meetings continue.

During the winter the evangelists went to Marshall County, into a neighborhood that seemed very dark spiritually. After one of the evening meetings there, in which he had preached with marvelous power, Brother Warner was passing out the door when a young rough gave him a kick. He turned and thanked the fellow and said he always praised God when he received such treatment. As he started on he received another kick, for which he also praised God aloud. At the house where he was stopping the sister had two very wicked sons. On the night the kicking occurred one of these young men, instead of retiring to bed, sat in his chair at the fireplace, his face in his hands, groaning. When asked what was the matter, he referred to what had happened that evening and said he felt sorry for Brother Warner, for surely he was a godly man, etc. When he saw how Brother Warner received such abuse, his heart was touched, and he was much pained. He and his brother had both mistreated Brother Warner and those with him and had in their presence cursed his mother for feeding them. When they saw the love manifested their hearts melted, and they became warm friends to the saints of God.

From Marshall County the company went up into Michigan, into Van Buren County. Here, at Geneva Center lived a young man whom the Lord had saved and was calling into the gospel work, Brother Barney E. Warren. The fact that he was under twenty-one years of age and that his father was unsaved and was opposed to his going into the ministry was an obstacle. But his father, who was a very wicked man, became very much convicted during the meetings held in a schoolhouse in the vicinity. He was seized with such trembling that in his attempt to steady himself by holding to the seats he shook the very floor of the building. Finally, in a consecration-meeting in Brother Joseph Smith's house, near Lacota, he rebelled against the Lord and started to leave the room. Before he reached the door the strength of his legs gave way and he sank instantly to the floor, and was unable to go farther. He then yielded. Brother Warner asked him if he was willing to let Barney go into the gospel work. His reply was, "Barney is the Lord's." The way was then opened for the young Brother Warren, and in the following April he became a part of the little singing company that should travel with Brother Warner for the next five years, and should consist of, besides Brother Warren, who was a bass singer, Sisters Nannie Kigar, Frances Miller, and Mother Smith. This constituted a complete quartet, with Brother Warner often reenforcing the tenor.

# The Harmony of Voices

### by

### John W. V. Smith

Excerpted from *Truth Marches On* (Anderson, Ind: Gospel Trumpet Company, Copyright © 1956).

# A Time to Remember: BEGINNINGS

**IT WOULD BE** hard to overestimate the significance of music in the spread of the movement in the early days. Warner himself was a composer of both music and lyrics and he also loved to sing. Many of the other early leaders had musical talents, too. It was no accident that the first book the Company published was a songbook, *Songs of Victory*. By 1900 four other songbooks had been issued. Most of the songs included were new and were written to fit the ideals and ideas of the movement. In the words of J. C. Fisher, editor of that first songbook, these songs were an expression of "the glorious light of liberty, grace, truth, and power the free and holy church has attained in this blessed evening light."

In 1886, the year following the appearance of *Songs of Victory*, Warner instituted a new evangelistic technique, the "company." This consisted of a party of four to six people who traveled together as a team of workers. The most obvious advantage of this arrangement was that it provided a group of singers. Warner's first company, consisting of Barney Warren, Nannie Kigar, Frances Miller, and "Mother" Sarah Smith, traveled together for over four years. Many other evangelists procured singers and organized their own companies. It might be noted in passing that this system provided an excellent opportunity for many young women to become active in evangelistic work.

One of the standard procedures was to drive into a town in a buggy or spring wagon, singing with all the strength the company could muster. They would drive up and down the streets of the town until a sufficient crowd had gathered to make an announcement about the meeting they were about to begin. In such a way they were able to attract many people who would not otherwise have attended. Many stories are told of singing in hotel lobbies, railroad stations, and other public gathering places.

More important than the fact that the early leaders were interested in music is the additional fact that the songs they composed were in truth lyrical expressions of the message they proclaimed. Titles like "The Church Triumphant," Brighter Days Are Sweetly Dawning," "He Sanctifies Me," and

"There's Music in My Soul," are loaded with theological overtones. Those who failed to respond to the spoken word often were led to make a commitment when the same message was set to music and sung by competent singers.

# The Flying Ministry

### by

### Herbert M. Riggle

Excerpted from *Pioneer Evangelism* (Anderson, Ind.: Gospel Trumpet Company, 1924).

**WHEN THIS** reformation work was in its infancy, we were constantly pushing out into new fields. All the ministers were inspired with the conviction that we are now engaged in the last great reformation that shall sweep over the earth before Christ's appearing. This work is the "great preparation" day, the bride being made ready for the coming of the Bridegroom. As we believe that this reformation restores to the Church the whole gospel in all its purity, then the responsibility to carry the saving message of truth to all nations becomes the greater. Imbued with this thought, the first preachers were a "flying ministry," disseminating the truth in every direction. Little attention was paid to the pastoral care of churches. Local elders and deacons were ordained in different congregations; but these were generally called and selected from each assembly, and were self-supporting. There was no system for pastoral support. We felt that our message was urgent, and that it was not wise to tarry too long in one place. Had the preachers classified as *evangelists* and *pastors*, I am sure nine-tenths would have registered *evangelists*.

As to the method of our early preaching, the reference system was generally followed. It was "precept upon precept; line upon line; here a little, and there a little." The sermons were mostly doctrinal, and this style was certainly effectual. Everything was proved by the Bible. This appealed to the people, and the remark was often heard, ''These folks prove every point of their doctrine from the Scriptures. They preach the Word.''

In large camp meetings it was customary to give out texts for others to read. This proved convenient, as the minister did not need to leaf through his Bible to find his Scripture proof text; when he desired it, he simply called out the chapter and verse and someone stood up and read it. The sermons were usually long, sometimes lasting two hours. It was remarkable, however, to see the people sit for hours apparently spellbound by their intense interest in the expounding of the Word of God.

There was much preaching from the prophecies and Revelation. Charts and blackboard illustrations were used by most of the ministers. This proved to be a very effectual method of presenting truth. It made their message appeal through the eye as well as the ear. The prophet said, ''Write it before them.''

The preaching was definite and radical. All manner of sin, false religion, and worldliness was exposed in the strongest terms. It was, ''Walk in the light, or go into darkness.'' This definite preaching separated the wheat from the chaff, and brought out a plain, spiritual people. Very often the minister, while presenting the strongest truth against apostate religions, would weep in the pulpit. This anointing of the Spirit, this melting power, this sowing in tears is what took hold of hearts with a mighty grip. The majority of the first preachers were very demonstrative in the pulpit. Sometimes in the midst of a sermon the minister (and most of the congregation) leaped and shouted for joy.

One of the greatest mistakes of my early ministry was to open up new fields of work and then rush off and leave them. For example, in Indiana County, Pennsylvania in the winter of 1893-94, we raised up several strong churches. They were our children in the Lord. The whole community was stirred for miles, and calls for meetings came in from every direction. Had I remained there for a few years and taken care of the tender flocks until capable pastors were raised up, and at the same time evangelized the surrounding communities, there would today be a mighty work to show the fruits of our labors. Instead of doing this, being one of the "flying ministry," I felt it my duty to hurry off to other new fields.

# Persecution

### by

### Herbert M. Riggle

Excerpted from *Pioneer Evangelism* (Anderson, Ind.: Gospel Trumpet Company, 1924).

**IT IS A FACT** all through the history of Christianity that when any one received additional light from God, and then had the courage to break away from some old, dead religious body and boldly declare his convictions, severe persecution followed. The lives of such men as Huss, Luther, Zwingli, Wesley, Alexander Campbell, and D. S. Warner attest this fact.

In the early years of the reformation movement in which we are engaged, there was intense opposition from every quarter. The definite message of true holiness, the one divine Church distinct from sectarian institutions, and that all sectarian religious bodies are unscriptural and are a part of Babylon out of which God is now calling his people back to Zion, stirred the ecclesiastical world in bitter hostility. In those days it was very common for mobs, headed by sectarian preachers, to attack our meetings.

At one place, during a camp meeting, a great rabble gathered and gave the brethren just five minutes to leave the grounds. Most of them did not have time to gather up their belongings. A few minutes after their departure the tents and tabernacle were blown to pieces with dynamite. One minister, to escape, walked a considerable distance through a stream of water.

# A Time to Remember: BEGINNINGS

While one of our brethren was conducting a meeting at Dawson, Pennsylvania, a crowd of the "baser sort" assembled with intent to kill the preacher. The building in which the services were being conducted was enclosed with half-inch siding. The pulpit was near one end of the building, and the preacher was standing near the wall while delivering the message. The mob secured a long, heavy pole. This they planned to thrust through the building at the brother. Providentially, no doubt, the preacher's pencil fell on the floor. The instant he stooped down to pick up his pencil, the pole, with terrific force, crashed through the wall and passed just over his head. Had he remained standing straight he probably would have been killed; at least he would have been severely injured.

It was no uncommon thing to be egged, stoned, and whipped. On one occasion while Brother Clayton was returning home from meeting, carrying a child in one arm and his bookcase in the other hand, a crowd of ruffians, urged on by professors of religion, attacked him with buggy whips and whipped him for some distance along the road. Under such ordeals the brethren usually praised God. In Illinois a wicked man kicked a brother who was praying in a corn patch, and compelled him to leave the field. A short time after, this man was killed by a lightning bolt on the same spot. In Pennsylvania a man struck one of the brethren a terrible blow in the face with his fist. The brother praised God and, turning the other side of his face, said, "You may strike that, too, if you wish." Instantly the offender fell down at the brother's feet, and said, "O God, I have struck a holy man! Please forgive me, and pray God to forgive me."

Personally we have had a taste of these things. I have been in mobs, have been struck over the head with canes and umbrellas, and have been cursed in the most abusive language. In every instance it has been by professed Christians. But when we read of the sufferings of Paul and others, we must conclude that the things we have been called to pass through are but "light afflictions." The sufferings of the present time do not compare with the glory that shall follow.

# My First Revival Meeting

## by

### Herbert M. Riggle

Excerpted from *Pioneer Evangelism* (Anderson, Ind.: Gospel Trumpet Company, 1924).

**IN THE LATTER** part of October, 1893, Wife and I launched out into the active work of the ministry, and from then until the present we have given our full time to the gospel work. A friend told us of a United Brethren church at North Point, Pennsylvania, in which we could hold meetings. He offered to take us in his buckboard buggy, the distance being thirty-eight miles. We packed our satchel and started over the hills on our first evangelistic tour. Our company consisted of Wife, our baby, and me. The people with whom we lodged made no profession of religion.

We continued this meeting for seventeen nights. The country was stirred for miles, and the attendance was very large. I had no older minister on whom to depend, therefore had to dig out my sermons upon my knees. I spent most of the time between meetings in prayer and the study of the Word. I have always thanked God for these experiences. Had I started out with older brethren, I would have depended much upon them to do the preaching and to bear the responsibility. As it was, we were thrown upon our own resources, and had to lean heavily upon God for wisdom and guidance.

A congregation of about thirty believers took their stand for the truth we preached. At one time seventeen members of the United Brethren denomination handed in their names to be taken from their church's class book. A goodly number of sinners were saved, and some believers sanctified. There was marked opposition from the sectarian element. They threatened to close the church house against us; but only two of the trustees favored this, while three stood in our favor. At the close of the meeting the new congregation withdrew to a hall offered freely by a merchant who was a non-professor of religion. This hall became the permanent place of worship for the brethren, until in later years a new church building was erected. This was my first revival-meeting.

# Through the Printed Page

### by

### Robert L. Berry

Excerpted from *Golden Jubilee Book* (Anderson, Ind.: Gospel Trumpet Company, 1931).

**THE STORY** of the *Gospel Trumpet* exhibits a series of dramatic vicissitudes and developments. Back in 1878 a little paper called the *Herald of Gospel Freedom* was started by the Northern Indiana Eldership, a split from the Winebrennarian Church of God. The year following, D. S. Warner, a member of the eldership, became associate editor, and the next year he was made editor. During the year 1880 the eldership arranged a consolidation of the *Herald* with the *Pilgrim*, which was published by G. Haines, and D. S. Warner became joint publisher with him. It was during this consolidation of two very small journals that D. S. Warner proposed that the name of the new paper be the *Gospel Trumpet*. This was agreed upon and two issues of the *Gospel Trumpet* were printed at Rome City, Indiana, and then the plant was moved to Indianapolis. After the stay of a year or more in Indianapolis, during which the Warner-Haines partnership was dissolved and J. C. Fisher became copublisher with D. S. Warner, the shop moved to Cardington, Ohio, and in May, 1883, it moved to Bucyrus, Ohio.

While the first appearance of the *Gospel Trumpet* seemed small, and indeed it was small, it had within it inherent powers of great expansion. It was no narrow program upon which it set out. It had for its object the bringing of salvation to sinners, of sanctification to believers, and the uniting of all true Christians in the one Church. Stupendous proposition for that day! But, like all true reformers, Daniel S. Warner never once was overcome by present harassing circumstances. He was supremely wrapped up in God and in the message he had from God to deliver. He trod through the world like a child of the Eternal King, and the little *Gospel Trumpet* carried a note of spiritual triumph unusual in religious papers.

In 1884 the tiny plant moved to Williamston, Michigan, where it remained until June, 1886, when it moved into Grand Junction, a town that never seemed to grow up, in southwestern Michigan.

The *Gospel Trumpet* had now been published for six years and was comparatively unknown. The circulation was small. But on removing to Grand Junction the work began to expand. It was in 1887 that E. E. Byrum, of Indiana, came to Grand Junction as publisher with D. S. Warner and took over the business management of the concern. He became managing editor, and D. S. Warner continued his evangelistic work. At once D. S. Warner gathered a company of four, all excellent singers, and began that series of annual evangelistic tours that planted the truth in many states.

Wherever this company went intense interest was aroused. Their singing had a profound effect. The preaching was so different, so astounding to so many, that it is not astonishing to know that the results were of so divergent a nature. While some rejoiced in the message and new-found spiritual freedom others were incensed and threatened mob violence. People who once heard this message of spiritual freedom never forgot it. While on his evangelistic tours D. S. Warner worked actively on the circulation of the paper, and his articles and news items were the most important features of the *Gospel Trumpet*.

During the twelve years that the *Gospel Trumpet* office and plant were at Grand Junction, Michigan, the progress was rapid. A songbook entitled *Anthems from the Throne* was issued in 1888. It contained 148 songs, 90 of which were set to music. It was edited by D. S. Warner and B. E. Warren.

# A Time to Remember: BEGINNINGS

During the year 1889 several tracts were published embracing such subjects as "The Church," "Millennium," "Marriage and Divorce," and the "Second Work of Grace."

A new wire-stitcher was added to the equipment in September of this year.

A Free-Tract Fund was first proposed in 1889. Previously to this time a few thousand tracts and about one hundred dollars worth of *Gospel Trumpet*s were sent out free each month.

In February, 1890, a new book, *Bible Readings,* was published. It consisted of various Bible subjects outlined, with scriptural references given. In March a stereotyping outfit was bought. In July D. S. Warner's book of poems was published under the title, *Poems of Grace and Truth.* The postage bill now amounted to two or three dollars a day. In December, 1890, a book—*Holiness Bible Subjects*—was issued. The author was H. C. Wickersham. It was similar to *Bible Readings* but contained the scriptural references in full. In the same year the famous tract—"Must We Sin? or a Conversation between Brother Light and Brother Foggy" was published and another one on the New Testament ordinances.

In January, 1891, the company began the publication of its first children's paper—*The Shining Light.* Its first editor was E. E. Byrum.

The *Gospel Trumpet* was made a weekly in 1892. The workers numbered nineteen. New tracts published were: "Questions and Answers on the Church," and "The Great Tobacco Sin." E. E. Byrum's new book, *Divine Healing of Soul and Body,* was issued in April.

It was in 1892 that the general camp meeting of the Church of God was held on the new camp grounds, one and one-half miles north of Grand Junction. Here a tabernacle forty by seventy feet was built in a grove of young trees.

During 1893 several new books were published, namely, *Biblical Trace of the Church, The Boy's Companion,* and a new songbook, *Echoes from Glory.* Other tracts were issued and in February of this year about one thousand tracts were sent out every day. Tracts and papers were sent all over the world. They were put on ocean vessels and carried to foreign countries.

Sometimes a tract or a *Gospel Trumpet* would be found by some honest hearts searching for more of God and they would rejoice in the new light which shone in upon their darkness. In this way many people first received their knowledge of truth and were led into the establishing grace of full salvation.

A great loss to the work was sustained in 1895. Daniel S. Warner, who had been editor from its beginning, was a man of God, tender as a woman but as bold as a lion. He lived and moved and had his being in the things of God. Besides his editorial duties he traveled extensively and left his imprint on thousands of hearts who never before had heard such preaching as came from his lips. People would be held spellbound while he preached for one, two, and sometimes three hours. His tenor voice carried a long distance. His form was emaciated and frail looking, but when he began to speak it seemed that his soul and mind were borne away into the heights of spiritual realities and the message came in glowing power.

On December 12 this great man rested from his labors. He laid down his armor, his pen, and departed to be with his Lord in Paradise. It seemed that he could not be spared, but while God's workmen fall, the work goes on. E. E. Byrum became editor on the death of D. S. Warner.

# The Trumpet Finds a Home

### by

### E. E. Byrum

Excerpted from *Life Experiences* (Anderson, Ind.: Gospel Trumpet Company, 1928).

**OUR FINANCIAL** struggles for thirty years after entering the publishing work was one of the principal factors in developing our faith. During that time we all worked without wages, donating our time for the furtherance of the gospel. Among the number were college men and women, many school teachers, and those having held responsible and remunerative positions which they were gladly willing to sacrifice to donate their service to help publish the gospel.

When I arrived at the office in the year 1887 there was an indebtedness of nearly six hundred dollars on the office building. This was considered a heavy indebtedness at that time, but it was paid in two or three years.

It was our intention to operate the business on a cash basis, which was done, with the exception of a few times during the eleven years at Grand Junction, Michigan. Sometimes when new machinery was purchased there would be an indebtedness for a few months.

At one time our bills kept increasing until the amount was about two thousand dollars. To many business houses this amount would be considered a trivial matter, but it was not so with us. We had no paid advertisements in our papers and books and did but little outside printing, consequently had to depend to quite an extent upon donations.

Every Monday night the employees met together in the capacity of a prayer meeting, where business affairs were presented, talks given concerning the needs of the work, and personal requests made known, then earnest prayers offered accordingly. Just before camp meeting that year we asked the Lord to help us out of debt before the close of the following month.

A man from Illinois came to the camp meeting and while there was impressed to make a donation of over two thousand dollars to the publishing work. At the time he was a stranger to us, but the Lord knew our needs and heard our petitions.

As the publishing work was rapidly increasing we were planning to erect a larger office building and a home building for lodging for the employees. Different plots of ground were selected upon which the buildings were to be erected, but we were never able to close a deal. Always something thwarted our efforts.

About this time we received a letter from Brother George Clayton, Moundsville, West Virginia, asking if we would consider moving our publishing plant to that city. He said that a shoe manufacturing company had failed and that their three-story brick building with all their shoe machinery and nearly two acres of land within the city limits was for sale and could be purchased for twenty-five hundred dollars. We could now begin to see that the Lord had prevented our purchasing lots for building in Grand Junction, which little village our business had outgrown.

In looking over the map to see just where Moundsville was located I remember placing the point of the pencil on the map and saying: "Here is about where we ought to be located." In looking to see what town was near we found that my pencil rested on Anderson, Indiana, although at that time we knew nothing about Anderson.

A few days later my brother, N. H. Byrum, accompanied me to Moundsville, and we made purchase of the property, paying ten dollars as we signed the contract, the remainder to be paid in sixty days. At that time we were having a struggle financially to meet the regular expenses of the publishing work. We began laying aside a certain amount each day as soon as we could conveniently do so. Many prayers were offered, and when the time came to make the payment there was a sufficient amount laid aside with only a few dollars left in the treasury.

Repairs were at once made on the building, and soon after the Grand Junction camp meeting, in June, 1898, with our special train of two passenger coaches, one baggage car, and nine freight cars heavily loaded, we left the little village and landed the next day in Moundsville, where we remained for eight years.

In the year 1905 arrangements were being made to erect a large office building beginning immediately after the camp meeting in June. At the annual meeting of the publishing company at the time of the camp meeting the subject was considered concerning a more central location.

The editor of the *Daily Echo,* in a news item, made a statement that the Trumpet Office may move, as the matter was under consideration by the members of the company. He did not believe that it was anything more than a rumor. A few days later we received a letter from the Chamber of Commerce, Anderson, Indiana, requesting us to locate in that city. They sent two men to Moundsville to investigate our business, who returned with a very satisfactory report.

About the first of September five officials of our company started on a tour to visit a number of cities in the central states to find a suitable location, but when they arrived at Anderson and saw the beautiful grove of about twenty acres and adjacent surroundings, they at once decided that they had found the proper location.

A few days later my brother and I returned to meet the owner of the land and make the purchase. The grove extended to the edge of the city limits and was an ideal spot for our work and for a camp ground. There were forty-four acres of land. The Chamber of Commerce sent a representative to us stating that they desired to have a part in helping us to locate. We consented to accept their kind offer and decided to give them something to do, as we could not remain long enough to look after all the details of the transaction.

We met with fifteen members of the Chamber of Commerce. A price for the land had been agreed upon but there were some adjustments of title to be made. A three-story brick building in the city was to be leased for five years for the publishing work; a sewer was to be extended to the new location, also a waterline, electricity, and telephone; arrangements were to be made with the school board for school privileges, all of which we placed in the hands of the Chamber of Commerce.

"What kind of a deal will this be?" they asked.

"It will be a cash deal."

"We may be ready to close the deal in a week. Will you be ready by that time?"

"Yes, sir, we will be ready."

At that time we only had four hundred dollars laid aside for that purpose, and the amount to be paid was nearly eight thousand dollars cash. But we had prayed and asked the direction of the Lord and felt that he would enable us to meet the requirements of any deal that we might feel led to make. They were delayed in making some of the adjustments necessary and in the meantime at the office at Moundsville every effort was being made to meet the coming requirements. It was the latter part of November before they notified us that all things were ready for settlement. Two or three days previously to this notice we had the full amount laid aside.

Upon arrival in Anderson again the deed and contracts were presented and after proper examination I wrote a check for nearly eight thousand dollars.

Large headlines appeared in the daily papers about the new publishing house and large corporation locating in the city.

On the first day of February, 1906, fourteen men from Moundsville came to Anderson and began the erection of the Trumpet Home building under the supervision of R. L. Byrum as contractor, who also employed other men from the city.

The following September the entire publishing plant and force of workers left Moundsville by special train. There were two passenger coaches and a baggage car. Twenty-six freight cars were loaded with machinery and publishing equipment.

# God's Colony in Man's World

### by

### Linfield Myers

Excerpted from *As I Recall . . . The Wilson-Morrison Years,* ed. by Larry G. Osnes (Anderson, Ind.: Anderson College Press, 1973).

**AFTER THE DEATH** of Warner in Grand Junction, Michigan, on December 12, 1895, a stock company known as the Gospel Trumpet Publishing Company was formed. Later, when the organization was quartered in Moundsville, West Virginia, all outstanding stock was recalled and cancelled, the Gospel Trumpet Publishing Company was dissolved, and the organization changed to a voluntary association having no capital stock. It was then incorporated as the Gospel Trumpet Company.

From time to time, as might be expected within a group of such dedicated people, areas of discord showed up. However, the original idea of D. S. Warner was never compromised and after his death the work went on under the able leadership of Enoch E. Byrum, who had in the meantime become editor of the periodical.

It was in 1898 that Moundsville, West Virginia, appeared to be a more advantageous location for the Gospel Trumpet Company. This time it required nine freight cars, two passenger coaches, and one baggage car to transport the workers and their worldly goods. The camp meeting, too, was moved to Moundsville along with the publication. The moves were not yet over, however, and the fruits of this small band of dedicated religionists were later to be felt more significantly in Indiana than in West Virginia.

The Anderson of those times was a bustling village and a fertile field for promoters. The Anderson Booster Club, which had been instrumental in reviving Anderson's flagging economy in the face of the double debacle of the loss of gas and the panic of 1907, had, in the course of its routine of contacting promising firms that might be enticed to Anderson, sent a brochure to the Gospel Trumpet Company of Moundsville, West Virginia, setting forth the attractions and advantages of the community. The Gospel Trumpet Company, while definitely not interested in any enticements offered its workers, glimpsed a new area of promise, mainly in the form of a tract of advantageously located acreage on high, level ground less than a mile from Anderson's courthouse. Unhappy with its situation in Moundsville, the firm considered the invitation from Anderson most opportune.

When the community discovered that the publishing house, as it was constituted in that particular era, was not an enterprise providing openings for an appreciable number of Anderson workers, but strictly an operation carried on by a colony of dedicated people who "lived-in" on company premises and were not paid wages or salaries as other people were, the development gave rise to second thoughts, particularly among the Anderson Park Place neighbors. The Gospel Trumpet Company workers comprised the more active nucleus of a religious sect not too easily understood by the great majority of Andersonians, to whom its members seemed, if anything, proponents of a throwback to various and sundry "fundamental" interpretations of the gospel which had been considered largely passé for decades. As one may well have guessed, the newcomers from West Virginia were regarded in Anderson as a group of religious fanatics. The community, in fact, rather pointedly left them alone. As time passed, however, concessions were made on both sides and Anderson eventually thawed out to the colony.

The Gospel Trumpet Company of Anderson prospered during the next decade and by 1917 the workers were put on an "allowance system" for the first time. As a result, many of the employees with families, long housed in the headquarters building which later became fondly known as "Old Main," were able to move off company property and into their own homes in the east side area.

The year 1917 brought another change to the religionists of Park Place, as the leadership, especially Joseph T. Wilson, then president of Gospel Trumpet Company, began thinking seriously about an idea he had considered for a number of years—the development of a school to train leaders to spread the gospel. The architects of the plan did not envision the educational phase of their work in the sense of a school but rather as a "finishing agency" for workers who had been tapped to convey the gospel.

The planners probably were not exempt from being torn by thoughts that (1) too-enlightened youth with their fresh but rebellious viewpoint might rock the boat too vigorously on work already started, and (2) that mere man is mortal, after all, and no individual can survive to carry his torch on earth forever. So it would be necessary to train new people, within limits, to extend the work. Other than that, there was just no appetite to get involved in academe.

The leaders in the thick of the struggle to survive in a hostile world had become so absorbed in the task of evangelism that they had given little consideration to education as any particular help toward that end. Coupled with this was the prevailing mood of the day of opposition to formal education for the ministry. This was in no sense a local situation; it was general. Indeed, along with other obvious problems, it might also have been something of a sign of the times that the Gospel Trumpet Company's movement leaned noticeably in the direction of anti-education.

Acceptance of the training school concept started, in consequence, pretty tentatively. While it is true that D. S. Warner and Enoch Byrum had each been to college, one could just about count on the fingers of one hand the pastors affiliated early with the Church of God reformation movement with college degrees. Church leaders in those trying times prior to World War I do not deny that they indeed did look upon the colleges and seminaries of the day as having "strayed far from the faith once delivered to the Saints." College degrees, if anything, seemed "self-seeking emblems of worldly sophistication." Admittedly, the climate for the start of the institution that was to become Anderson College was not precisely salubrious.

In 1917, Joseph T. Wilson, the principal proponent of the educational idea, assumed charge of the "school department" of the Gospel Trumpet Company. He had two full-time teachers, Henry C. Clausen and Mabel Helms, and he recruited three others to assist in the instructional chores, including Russell R. Byrum, the latter's wife Bessie Byrum, and H. A. Sherwood. There were fewer than fifty students enrolled the first year. Admission was mostly a matter of desire and dedication. Preparatory school and scholastic achievement meant nothing; in fact, an eighth-grade education was sufficient. Tuition was no problem for the avowed gospel worker. Others had to pay the munificent sum of three dollars per course. Room rent in quarters vacated by the workers was one dollar and fifty cents to two dollars per week. Food was the biggest item in the student budget—up to three dollars a week—but even there special arrangements could probably have been made. And imagine, a student could enter the school at any time, even though being present for the start of the October term was "recommended."

Meanwhile there was a war on in Europe into which America was inexorably drawn. Indeed, after its first year of operation, many of the Anderson Bible Training School's young men marched off to do their part to make the world safe for democracy. Classes shrank; gloom pervaded all. Even more serious, the school operation had incurred enough deficits to pose a very real financial threat to the Gospel Trumpet Company.

The life of the school hung by a slender thread, but Wilson went determinedly ahead with the second term of the venture in education. It was his dogged determination that kept the school alive for the next two years. The end of the conflict across the Atlantic suddenly opened new vistas in church expansion and there was a shortage of experienced leadership in the church. Wilson needed to be across the street at the publishing house instead of trying to conduct a school!

It was on February 10, 1919, that Wilson addressed a letter to John Arch Morrison, just turned twenty-three, who had been named pastor of a little church in Delta, Colorado, asking him about his qualifications as a teacher, and if he would consider a different kind of "call" to Anderson, Indiana.

# The Missionary Home

### by

### Charles E. Brown

Excerpted from *When the Trumpet Sounded* (Anderson, Ind.: The Warner Press, Copyright © 1951).

**THE FIRST** preachers were nearly all farmers, or at least countrymen, miners, and the like. The first Church of God preachers seemed to shun the towns and cities. Most of their meetings were held in country schoolhouses impossible to identify today. But while Warner was preaching in San Diego back in 1893, he seems to have got the vision of city work, and he recommended to his followers that they enter the cities and start working there. This course they followed almost immediately.

At first they often opened rescue missions among the lowest, the vilest, and the neediest. This was not always the case. Sometimes they simply went where they could and held meetings in the homes and cottages of the working people among whom they moved. It was not long until there were so many preachers in the larger towns that it was desirable to build missionary homes to shelter them. These missionary homes sprang up almost overnight all across the nation. In 1910 there were nineteen of them dotted across the United States from the Atlantic to the Pacific. To them any recognized minister of the Church of God could go and expect hospitality at any time. Many of these homes provided facilities for study and the training of young workers. They were, in fact, substitutes for the theological schools.

The missionary homes followed the example of the Trumpet Home, where the Gospel Trumpet workers gave their services free and were housed by the Company. In their leisure time and sometimes during work hours classes in a great many different subjects were held. The missionary homes, too, often held classes, and the leaders gave the workers guidance and training in practical home missionary and preaching work.

Almost as fast as they came, the missionary homes disappeared. The famous missionary home at 700 West 74th Street in Chicago housed for many years as many as twenty-five gospel workers at a time. This home remained open until 1922, when it was closed, the furnishings sold, and the home leased as a rooming house and apartments. Probably this home and the one in New York City held out the longest, for it is quite certain that very few others remained open so long. The missionary home and workers had, in fact, in nearly every case gathered a large congregation. The superintendent of the home became the pastor of the congregation, and the home was turned into a parsonage or sold or leased that the income from it might furnish a parsonage for the pastor.

# The Floating Bethel

## by

## Isham E. ("Joe") Crane

Excerpted from *Missions of the Church of God,* September 1968.

**IT WAS STARTED** in 1893 with the spring flood on the Ohio River. A large coal barge broke loose from its moorings to a tugboat and drifted down the river until it wrecked on the high ground of an island. The bulkhead was badly damaged, and the barge was left for the nearby residents to salvage the coal for their own use.

In the meantime a traveling evangelist was in Canada assisting several young congregations. Returning to his home area in West Virginia along the Ohio River, he announced his plan for the new mission venture. He would purchase the wrecked barge, rebuild the bulkhead, jack up the barge, and place rollers under it to move it into the river. The barge was purchased for twenty dollars. The father and his eldest son worked all summer to repair the boat and drift it down river where carpenters could construct the superstructure.

The remodeled riverboat was not luxurious; however, it was sturdy and large, providing living quarters for the families of the gospel workers and a large room for church services. The boat had no motor; therefore, it had to be towed upstream and allowed to drift down to chosen landing spots where the evangelist and gospel workers performed their mission.

At the turn of the century, the industrial revolution was opening up the Ohio River basin to rapid population growth.

# A Time to Remember: BEGINNINGS

Many people were making new homes in the towns and cities up and down the big river. The purpose of the *Floating Bethel* was to announce that this new and rapidly expanding territory was God's mission land. The church as the house of God was to be a mobile mission serving the communities.

The river church boat would tie up to a dock or find mooring at a spot accessible to the working people or near the central business district. The usual procedure was to observe the time of day when factory workers were leaving their jobs and to have a musical group on top of the boat's superstructure, singing gospel songs and announcing that religious services would be held on the *Floating Bethel* that evening and on Sunday. Often the sanctuary, seating nearly three hundred, would be filled for the preaching services.

In several communities a number of families were converted, and they provided the nucleus of local congregations. When the church boat continued on its mission downstream, a beginning congregation remained in the community.

An enriching fellowship grew among the evangelist's family and the other members of the gospel team as they shared in this new kind of mission. There is always a joy in serving people with the good news even among hardships and trials, not to speak of inconveniences like having to wait for the right flow of the river current. The workers dispensed Christian literature, visited on shore, and sang the gospel in addition to conducting church services.

What was the result of the river church boat ministry? Through the *Floating Bethel,* over forty congregations were established along the Ohio River in West Virginia, Pennsylvania, and Ohio, reports W. H. Clayton, son of G. T. Clayton, owner, builder, and pastor of the *Floating Bethel.* The ministry of the *Floating Bethel* came to an end in 1898 when the boat was destroyed by fire. Later the boat was dismantled and the material used in construction on the Clayton farm.

The story of the *Floating Bethel* portrays the spirit of urgency that lives in the church and that will discover effective ways of delivering the story of Christ to the contemporary world.

# California

### by

### Robert L. Berry

Berry's accounts in this section are quoted from the *Golden Jubilee Book* (Anderson, Ind.: Gospel Trumpet Company, 1931).

**J. W. BYERS,** with his faithful wife, Jennie, began the work in California. On November 15, 1890, they landed in San Diego, California, strangers in a strange land. A holiness mission superintendent opened his pulpit for Brother Byers. Later a tent was bought and used. Then a church building was rented and Samuel Good and his wife donated a house and lot and it was remodeled into the first church building owned by the Church of God in California. At the call of J. D. Hatch, a blacksmith, and later a minister and missionary to Japan, the Byers' moved to Los Angeles, where for months on end revival went on. In 1892 D. S. Warner went west and his first camp meeting was held in Los Angeles that year. "At one of our Sunday services," Brother Byers writes, "Brother Warner preached three sermons of three hours each." Nine hours of sermon! Those who ever heard D. S. Warner know why those hours passed quickly. Later on the work spread to other sections.

# Indiana

by

## Robert L. Berry

**INDIANA** might be called the birthplace of the publishing work. The first copy of the *Gospel Trumpet* came from Rome City, Indiana, in January, 1881. After two issues it was moved to Indianapolis, No. 70 North Illinois Street. At this time D. S. Warner, the editor, said:

"We are experiencing that it takes a man wonderfully burned out for God to publish a paper that is simply true to Jesus and up to the Bible standard of salvation from all sin. A thousand points of expediency and policy must be disregarded, and the eye fixed on God alone. O reader, you that love God and the truth, do not forget to pray for us."

The Byrums—E. E. and N. H.—came from near Union City, Indiana, but their pioneer work was done in Michigan in connection with the *Gospel Trumpet*.

It was near Akron, Indiana, at a church near a place called Beaver Dam, that D. S. Warner and five others severed their connection with the Northern Indiana Eldership in 1881. From this time and place the work spread to many places in this state. David Leininger was one of the pioneers here. The first camp meeting was held near Beaver Dam in 1887. In 1896 the land was bought which is now the Yellow Creek Lake camp ground.

# Kansas

by

## Robert L. Berry

**D. S. WARNER** and company began the work in Kansas, the first meeting being a tent meeting near Winfield on the Aldrich farm in 1886. The next year the same company held a meeting near Chanute, where Mary J. Sweeney first heard the message. She had been healed after more than nine years of invalidism. The Warner gospel party also held a meeting at Galesburg, the home of Dr. S. G. Bryant. A year or two later Mary Cole and Lodema Kaser and their gospel party held a meeting at Galesburg and Dr. Bryant was saved. He gave up his practice and became one of the pioneer ministers of the state, carrying the message everywhere. In 1890 D. S. Warner was at Wichita at a kind of state camp meeting. This was the foundation meeting. Out of it came several ministers, and the light of God never went out. Cornelia Bateman, a colored woman who saw clearly the true Church, kept the work going in Wichita when the white people had given up. Later the white brethren took courage and began again. This time it was carried to permanent success. Prominent among the pioneers were Samuel McAlister, Dr. Bryant, S. M. Helm, and Charles Bright. Mary Cole and her party, J. E. Roberts and J. L. Green, did much work there. Nora I. Lee and Sister Sweeney were pillars in the Chanute church.

# Kentucky

### by

### Charles E. Brown

Excerpted from *When the Trumpet Sounded* (Anderson, Ind.: The Warner Press, Copyright © 1951).

**THE BEGINNING** of the Kentucky work is dated by W. Thomas Carter (born 1867) as in 1892. The place was at the L and E Railway junction just six miles east of Winchester, where the state campground is now located. It seems that in this village a few families of believers in holiness were conducting cottage prayer meetings. They sent for a sample copy of every holiness paper published in the United States and finally decided that they would all subscribe for a holiness paper, but since they belonged to four different denominations, it should be a nonsectarian paper. Therefore they selected the *Gospel Trumpet* and six families subscribed for it. After reading the *Trumpet* awhile they wrote for some of the ministers to come and hold a meeting. When Carter read in the *Gospel Trumpet* that A. J. Kilpatrick and J. N. Howard were preparing to go to Kentucky, he write to Kilpatrick to know if they would need any help in singing. In reply Kilpatrick wrote that if Carter could pay his own fare and get there, they would be glad to have him with them. Carter considered this a starting point, so he arranged to go. He had enough money to pay the fare by purchasing a broker's (that is, a cut-rate) ticket to Cincinnati. There he stayed overnight high up in an attic because it was cheap. Next day, April 27, 1892, he arrived at Dodge, a place between Winchester and Mount Sterling, and joined Kilpatrick and Howard in the first meeting held in the state by Church of God ministers in the present reform.

The meeting was a success; the attendance was good; and though not very many were saved, quite a number declared themselves out of all sectarian division and took their stand with the reformation. Carter returned to this town the next summer in company with Kilpatrick, and they had a good meeting. A few were saved and the church better established. When the meeting closed James Flynn invited the evangelists to Mount Sterling, where he lived, and they held two services in the courthouse there.

# Louisiana

### by

### M. LaVerne Norris

Excerpted from ''The Church of God in Louisiana: A Sociological Study of Its Structure and Function.'' (Master's Thesis) Louisiana State University: 1952.

**JEREMIAH COLE** and W. W. Bradley were the first Church of God preachers to evangelize Louisiana. In 1893 these men preached at a little Baptist church near Hammond, Louisiana, where services were held for about three years. It is Robert H. Owens, however, who came to Louisiana in 1894 or 1895, who is credited with being directly responsible for the beginning of practically all the present church work in Louisiana. Frellsen F. Smith, in an article appearing in a 1935 issue of the *Gospel Trumpet,* gives a brief account of the life and works of Owens.

In the closing year of the Civil War, 1865, Owens was born on a farm near Walnut Grove, Mississippi. Because of the poor health of his father, Robert, the eldest son, was given the responsibility of providing for the family at an early age. Despite this, however, he was able to reach the sixth grade in his studies. At the age of seventeen, Owens became a Christian and was actively engaged in church work for about a year. At the end of the year he found himself without a religious experience. His conduct for the next seven years—drinking, swearing, fighting, and raising all manner of disturbances throughout the country—won for him the title of "Fighting Bob." A year or two of this time was spent at Lena Station, Louisiana. In 1890 Owens returned to his father's home, found that his father had become a Christian, and he himself was soon converted in a meeting under the preaching of D. S. Warner. Owens immediately began studying the Bible, because he felt God had called him to preach. He preached with great success in his hometown and other places in Mississippi for the next few years, and then in 1899 he returned to Lena Station, Louisiana, where he also met with success. This was the beginning of what is now the Sharp Church of God. During Owens' first meeting in Louisiana, W. F. Ward, at that time a Baptist minister, studied the Bible to refute the teachings of Owens. Instead, he convinced himself of the truth of the doctrine, accepted Owens' teachings, and entered the Church of God ministry in 1894. Ward became one of the leading pioneers in the work in Louisiana. During the more than forty-five years that Owens served in the active ministry of the church, a number of other successful ministers accepted the message under his preaching.

# Michigan

by

### Robert L. Berry

**FOR SEVERAL** years the *Gospel Trumpet* office was in Grand Junction and the general camp meeting was held there. J. C. and Allie R. Fisher were pioneers in the ministry in Michigan. Mrs. A. B. Palmer, who was healed of blindness at a meeting at Bangor, states that just before her healing Brother Fisher was so earnest about it that he was as one dead for some time. When the time came for prayer her eyes were instantly opened. The voice of D. S. Warner was heard in this community for years, and there his remains now lie. Sebastian Michels, Wm. N. Smith, and others began to preach. The work was begun in Kalamazoo by Sebastian Michels and soon it fell to Wm. Hartman, who has held one of the longest pastorates of anyone in the country. Several cases of miraculous healing attended the beginning of the work in Kalamazoo. The old church house is still there. From the southwest part of Michigan the work spread to all the state.

# Minnesota

by

### Anna E. Koglin

Excerpted from *History of the Church of God in Minnesota,* Copyright © 1976 by Anna E. Koglin.

**THE MESSAGE** reached northern Minnesota in 1896. In 1895 James B. Peterman, in Spokane, Washington, received a *Gospel Trumpet* which he shared with his brother and his pastor, George W. Bailey. After reading a few issues they declared themselves free from all sectarianism and in unity with all God's people everywhere. They found the message which they had received through the *Gospel Trumpet* of such a compelling nature that Bailey with his family and James B. Peterman were soon headed east. They were driving a four-horse wagon over mountains and plains in the direction of Grand Forks, North Dakota, on the North Dakota-Minnesota boundary.

In 1896 C. H. Tubbs and his wife Mary arrived in Grand Forks in response to the directive of D. S. Warner to "proceed West." After helping briefly with the work in Grand Forks, Brother Tubbs "proceeded" into Minnesota. One day after he had prayed for guidance to be led to some souls hungry for the gospel he boarded the train which would cross the Red River into Minnesota. He got off at Melvin, forty-five miles distant, and walked in the direction he felt God leading him. Seeing a certain farm home he felt this was the home to which God was sending him. He walked up to the door. Mrs. H. B. Hafterson greeted him. After explaining salvation and the Christian life to Mr. and Mrs. Hafterson they knelt in prayer and the couple was gloriously saved. The Haftersons were loyal followers of Christ to the end of their long lives. (Brother Hafterson lived to be 96 years old.) A sister of Mrs. Hafterson, "Aunt Mary," was soon converted, too. These three people put their Christianity into action immediately. They subscribed to the *Gospel Trumpet,* were baptized (in a creek near their home), attended the camp and assembly meetings in Grand Forks, and instituted family worship and Sunday school in their home. (There was no other Sunday school in their community until 1935). A few years later, in 1908, when Zeno Newell held some meetings in the home of Mary Hafterson in Melvin, a number of persons were converted and an ordinance meeting was held in which nineteen took part.

C. H. Tubbs also felt called to other points in Minnesota in the year 1896. He visited in the homes and held evangelistic meetings in Mentor (a small town on the shores of Maple Lake, Polk County). He also preached in Moorhead. The results of these two efforts have not been recorded.

Some rather far-reaching results followed the efforts of James

# A Time to Remember: BEGINNINGS

Peterman (one of the missioners to Grand Forks) and W. J. Baldwin, when in 1899 they visited a home in rural Thief River Falls, Minnesota (about sixty miles from Grand Forks). This was the home of the August Koglin family, the parental home of the present writer. My parents had been saved in the Evangelical Association, but the message of sanctification and victory over sin, and the outgoing concern of the evangelists, filled their hearts with confidence and great gladness. The very next summer my parents attended the camp meeting in Grand Forks and took me along. As the years went by other members of the growing family had their turn to attend the camp meeting. Those who were not saved at home found relationship with Christ at the altar of the camp meeting and all were baptized in the Red River. Several members of the family have filled places of responsibility in the Church of God, even in foreign countries. In 1896 S. O. Susag preached in Sunberg where an enthusiastic group was formed and later united with the Willmar congregation.

In the following decade the message of the Church of God is carried to a number of towns, cities, and country places. In 1900 we see D. O. Teasley preaching in Duluth and being assisted in house-to-house calling by an enthusiastic layman. In 1902 the first camp meeting of the Church of God in Minnesota is held in the Hawick-Paynesville area, with Enos and Elihu Key, C. H. and Mary Tubbs, and S. O. and Martha Susag as ministers. It appears that the Key brothers having come up from Indiana, had preached in this area even before 1902 and had readied the people for a camp meeting. In 1903 Thomas Nelson moved his printing equipment for publishing Scandinavian literature from Grand Forks to St. Paul Park, and a lively congregation of the church came into existence.

# Ohio

## by

### Robert L. Berry

**IN THE DISTRICT** around Payne the evening light message first took root in Ohio. J. N. Howard received entire sanctification and light on the church question at the same time and later heard D. S. Warner expound the truth more perfectly. John S. Byers, father of Charles E. Byers, pastor at Springfield, was one of the pioneers. A. J. Kilpatrick was perhaps the most influential of the early Ohio pioneers and B. E. Warren, William G. Schell, and C. W. Naylor were not far behind. Brother Kilpatrick was a heavyset Irishman, very precise in his statements, and noted for his common sense. It is told of him that once a congregation sent for him to settle a matter that was about to divide them. It seems a brother had married a second wife too soon after the death of his first one to please some of them and some were for turning him out of the church. When all the participants were collected Brother Kilpatrick said: "Ahem! What is it that you are troubled about?" They told him. "Well," he said, "we shall let the Scripture settle it. The Bible says: 'For the woman . . . is bound by the law to her husband so long as he liveth; but if the husband be dead, she is loosed from the law of her husband. So then if, while her husband liveth, she be married to another man, she shall be called an adulteress: but if her husband be dead, she is free from that law; so that she is no adulteress, though she be married to another man' (Rom. 7:2-3). Now, brethren, I want to ask a question— 'Is the woman dead?' " Upon their informing him that the man's wife was dead, Brother Kilpatrick said: "Well then, that settles it. Good-bye." A great deal of trouble might be eliminated if the Word of God were allowed to settle it.

The first services near Springfield were held at the Black Horse schoolhouse about two miles west of town and about one west of the Ohio State camp grounds was erected the first house of worship, a small structure about twenty-by-thirty feet. Later a larger one, about thirty-by-fifty feet, was built. B. E. Warren lived here for several years and there was a good congregation.

Later the truth spread into all parts of Ohio and it is today better evangelized than any state.

# Oregon

## by

### Donald D. Johnson

Excerpted from "An Historical Survey of the Church of God in the Pacific Northwest." (Master's Thesis) Anderson School of Theology: 1955.

**THE ARRIVAL** of John L. Green in Woodburn, October 30, 1893, is generally supposed to mark the beginning of the Church of God reformation in Oregon. However, as early as 1890, one family of Church of God people by the name of Armstrong had moved to Woodburn. The writer has obtained the following account concerning these early Church of God people from Mrs. Nora (Armstrong) Tooker, daughter of Mr. and Mrs. Alexander H. Armstrong, who was a child of nine when they moved to Oregon (a personal letter dated March 7, 1955):

> My parents, Mr. and Mrs. Alexander H. Armstrong, sold their farm in Washington Co., Kansas and bought a farm 4 miles from Woodburn, Oregon in 1890. My grandparents, Mr. and Mrs. J. C. Green, sold their farm in Eastern Kansas and bought a farm near father's place. My grandparents had heard the truth concerning holiness, sanctification, divine healing, sectism, and the Church of God from Brother George and Sister Mary Cole, Lodema

**100**

Caser, Brother Hayner, and Brother James
Willis who had come from the East and held a
six- or eight-weeks' meeting in a tabernacle in
grandfather's grove in Kansas. . . . When
Grandfather Green came to Oregon he and
father read the Bible and studied Scripture
daily, to see if this was Bible doctrine. Father
was so interested he and grandfather sent money
to James Willis asking would he come to
Oregon and hold a meeting. He came in January
1891. I remember distinctly, father carried my
little sister and mother carried the baby. And
both carried lanterns and umbrellas thro a dense
woods and a very bad wagon road. I was nine
years old. With a lantern and umbrella we went
to the schoolhouse to hear Brother Willis
preach. For several weeks we did not miss a
night. I do not recall any conversions, and no
healings, or baptisms in this meeting, and
Brother Willis returned East.

My father died in 1892 and my grandparents
went to Western Kansas. Before that a Brother
and Sister Clark and Brother and Sister William
Snavely from Missouri came to Woodburn.
Meetings were held in my (widowed) mother's
home in town. The five of them would laugh,
and shout and sing. These were to my
knowledge the only Church of God people in
Oregon or Washington at that time. Mother took
us children back to Western Kansas.

About this time (1892) an elderly couple, ''Grandpa'' and
''Grandma'' Reed, had moved to Oregon from Illinois and were
living in Albany.

After the return of J. C. and Phoebe Green and Mrs.
Armstrong and her family to Kansas, J. L. Green, son of J. C.
and Phoebe Green, felt led of God to go to Oregon. This was in

the year 1893. He and his wife arrived in Woodburn which was probably due to his parents having lived there a year or so prior to that date. From this time Oregon was never without Church of God ministers, evangelists, and gospel workers.

# Pennsylvania

### by

### Robert L. Berry

**IT IS REMARKABLE** what will come from the smallest beginnings. George T. Clayton and company first carried our message into Pennsylvania. Under their labors Herbert M. Riggle was converted and later joined them in the work.

One day James S. McCreary was walking down one of Pittsburgh's streets when his eyes fell on a tract in the street. On picking it up he read "Floating Bethel—Sixth Street Wharf." He attended a service which happened to be an ordinance service and his heart was warmed and filled. In a few months he went to Grand Junction, Michigan, where he was baptized. On returning to Pittsburgh he began services in his home at 5903 Broad Street. Three persons attended. But it grew. Every Sunday someone was saved or healed. When the house was too small a hall was rented. Later A. T. Rowe became pastor. There is an established congregation in Pittsburgh today.

The first congregation in the state was established in Indiana County. In a few years a camp meeting was established at Emlenton, Pennsylvania, which is one of the largest camp meetings in the United States. I. S. McCoy, a coal miner, became a soul winner, and did much pioneer work. We must mention J. H. Rupert, John L. Williams, J. Grant Anderson, Charles E. Brown, John C. Blaney, and William Drew, among the pioneers of the work in Pennsylvania. William J. Paxton was saved on the *Floating Bethel*.

# Beginnings of Our Missionary Work

## by

### Frederick G. Smith

Excerpted from *Look on the Fields* (Anderson, Ind.: Missionary Board of the Church of God, 1920).

**IN THE EARLY** part of this religious movement the character of the work accomplished was reformative rather than missionary, attention being given almost exclusively to the correction of errors and abuses that had arisen in connection with historic Christianity. Within a few years, however, the scope of the movement began to widen. God began to impress upon his ministers the fact that in addition to being reformers working on the basis of a Christian civilization, they must also, if they were to be truly apostolic, become *missionary* in character, by laboring to plant the Christian faith in the "regions beyond."

A number of ministers made their way to England and some of the Continental countries; but since these particular countries are not missionary fields, we must regard the efforts put forth as evangelistic, the same as if performed in our own country.

About the first circumstance in the series of events that began to awaken the church to the needs of the heathen lands occurred in the year 1897. At that time a terrible famine was raging in India and the sympathies of the American people were aroused. The brethren raised a liberal contribution, and then sent a representative to India to see that it was properly distributed. About that time, or perhaps a year earlier, Brother John A. D. Kahn, who was a student in the Calcutta University, received a catalog from the Gospel Trumpet Company and purchased some of the literature. Correspondence between him and some of the brethren in America developed, and in 1897 we sent over a half-ton of books and tracts for distribution in India; we also sent two small printing presses. Brother Kahn began publishing a paper.

In 1903 Brother Kahn visited the United States. While here he wrote a book entitled *India's Millions*. His writings and sermons did much to create missionary interest and zeal in the churches. When he returned to India, in 1904, Brother George W. Bailey and wife, and Sister N. Evalyn Nichols, of Washington, went with him as missionaries. Brother E. E. Byrum also accompanied them to India on his trip around the world, investigating conditions and seeking missionary openings. A number of other brethren were also instrumental in stirring up the church in the interest of missions, and soon a number of missionaries were at work in different countries. In January, 1910, the first number of the *Missionary Herald* appeared, and this magazine accomplished a splendid work, but after two years it was discontinued, the missionary subject-matter being transferred to a special department of the *Gospel Trumpet*.

Experience soon proved that the practice of missionaries going out to various countries on their own responsibility and then appealing to the home church for support was not satisfactory. The need of responsible oversight of this phase of the church's work was so keenly felt that at the general camp meeting of the Church of God, held at Anderson, Indiana, in June, 1909, the ministerial assembly chose seven brethren to act as a missionary board, with the duty of ''advising, instructing, encouraging, or restraining those who feel called to the foreign missionary field.''

# Eastern Canada

### by

### Beverly C. Anderson

Excerpted from ''A History of the Church of God in Ontario, 1882-1955.'' (Master's Thesis) Anderson School of Theology: 1955.

**THE CHURCH OF GOD** movement generally recognizes 1881 as the year of its beginning. However, it was not until 1889 that D. S. Warner and company crossed the Niagara River and went into Canada to denounce "sectism" and declare the "true gospel."

This was not the first contact made in Ontario by the Church of God movement. It was through another area of evangelism, that of the printed page, that the "truth" first came to this as well as many other parts of the world. The *Gospel Trumpet* had a very significant part in carrying the message of the "true Church," and was often already being read by some people in the communities before these evangelistic teams arrived to hold gospel meetings.

The first person in Ontario to have any correspondence published in the *Gospel Trumpet* was a woman lay preacher by the name of Mrs. Eliza J. White. She received her first copies of the *Gospel Trumpet* at least by 1882, at which time it was only in its second year of publication. Here is part of that letter (published in the *Gospel Trumpet,* February 15, 1883):

> We received your paper three times, so far like it very well. My husband, myself, and a few others are outside of denominations, have been so for about two years, cannot submit to idolatry and man's yoke . . . We meet in private houses excepting one place where is built a hall for us to worship in. Pray for us that we may stand firm for God's truth and that nothing of the world be bound upon us, that our master be but one, and that the great God of heaven.

It was into these conditions that the Warner party came, in November, 1888. The party consisted of D. S. Warner, B. E. Warren, Mother Sarah Smith, Frankie Miller, and Nannie Kigar. Apparently Warner had reached Ontario before the rest of the group, for B. E. Warren in his letter to the *Gospel Trumpet* (December 15, 1888) wrote,

> We arrived at Welland November 24, when we met dear Brother Warner whom we had been absent from for some time. We also met Brothers Becken and Thomas, who conveyed us to their homes a distance of about eight miles. . . . We have commenced our meeting in Fenwick, Ontario.

In a later issue of the *Gospel Trumpet* (January 1, 1889) is a letter from D. S. Warner, in which he states the condition of this group of saints in Ontario.

> We had only corresponded with Brother John E. Smith of this place, and had not much idea of the stage of progress the work had attained here. But we are happy to say that we found more dear saints here than we had expected. The numbers of the names of the saints in this place are about twenty. A few good souls have come to the meeting from other points and we hear of little groups scattered about in several places. But we found the dear ones in this place much discouraged and scattered and some had entirely let go their confidence, and but very few were fully clear.

Warner and company remained in the Niagara Peninsula until March, 1889, holding evangelistic meetings. In Fenwick the meetings were held in an unheated hall over Nunn's blacksmith and wagon shop. A meeting was next held in Crowland, where they were allowed to use a "comfortable house of worship." A meeting was held at St. Ann, and in correspondence from this place Warner spoke of other groups farther west which he did not visit.

Before Warner and company left Ontario they accomplished a few things that would give some stability to the various groups. Warner stated in one of his letters that he had obtained over forty subscribers for the *Trumpet* since being in Canada. Some plans were made also for a camp meeting during the summer. Warner also told in one of his letters of ordaining leaders to carry on the work in Ontario after a meeting in Crowland.

At the time of Warner's departure there were three congregations—Crowland, Welland, and Fenwick—holding services regularly, each group numbering between twelve and eighteen. There were other isolated saints at various points within the general area, the Kaumeyers of Chippawa being perhaps the most widely known.

# Western Canada

### by

### H. C. Heffren

Excerpted from *Voices of the Pioneers* (Camrose, Alta.: The Camrose Canadian, 1970).

**IN 1906** Karl Arbeiter from North Dakota came to Winnipeg and started a German-language congregation of the Church of God which has persevered ever since. The congregation at Plum Coulee, Manitoba began in 1914 when Gottlieb Butgereit held meetings there. It was then that the Unger family became affiliated with the church. Later on the Walkofs joined the fellowship and they were instrumental in starting the work in Morden. Originally these congregations all held services in the German language but as time passed the Plum Coulee group phased into English, followed by Morden. In Winnipeg there is a congregation in each language. Just as the Ontario churches received help from nearby states so Manitoba drew evangelists from Minnesota and North Dakota. Early pioneers included frequent visits from S. O. Susag, as well as Jonas Ratzlaff and Gottlieb Arbeiter. When Karl Arbeiter was advanced in years he developed a cancer which was so serious the doctors refused to operate. He was sent home to die, but in answer to prayer he was miraculously healed and lived many more years.

## A Time to Remember: BEGINNINGS

Meanwhile the burgeoning young city of Edmonton was hearing the message from another source. A young colored minister named W. H. Smith arrived from Denver, Colorado and was soon attracting great crowds of listeners. In 1905 Edmonton was not a very large place. Alberta had just become a Province that year. Although Edmonton was chosen as the capital it was only a fringe town serving as a trading center for fur traders and settlers. There were no paved streets or street cars and only board sidewalks. Early settlers relate stories of shooting ducks in a large pond very close to where the present Tegler Building stands. The northern C.P.R. terminal was Strathcona, named after Lord Strathcona. The high level bridge was not built until 1911 so most of the river traffic was handled by a ferry which operated near where the present 105th Street bridge is located. A few fairly large river barges plied up and down stream hauling freight.

Jasper Avenue was the main thoroughfare and it soon showed signs of major development. A pile of stones and building materials occupied the present site of the Royal Bank building. It was here that W. H. Smith conducted street meetings. Evangelist Smith possessed great personal charm which enabled him to make friends. He was a gifted speaker and . . . could sing well. Although he was single he was an expert cook as well as a good gardener. Crowds of people were attracted on Jasper Avenue to listen to this earnest man proclaim the gospel, after which he would invite his listeners to attend the evening meeting at the mission.

The Mission referred to was a property that was located on 96th Street and 114th Avenue. Missions were common in the early days of the church. Almost all major centers had a mission. It was usually a large building with a commodious hall which provided for meetings and with living quarters for the pastor. Several additional rooms served to accommodate itinerant evangelists or gospel workers when they were not holding meetings elsewhere. Thus the mission served as a church and an unofficial headquarters from which to direct efforts to surrounding districts, as well as a shelter for those who had no permanent home or congregation to support them.

In those days no collections were taken, no salary was provided, and the income of gospel workers was entirely supplied through what is now called "trusting in the Lord."

# Mexico

### by

### B. F. Elliott

Excerpted from *Experiences in the Gospel Work in Lower California, Mexico* (La Paz, Baja, Calif.: The Gospel, 1906).

**IT WAS,** I think, in the year 1891, while preaching on the street of Santa Barbara, California, the writer was impressed with the great need of the gospel being carried to the Spanish-speaking people of Mexico (Baja, California). More and more was this burden laid upon his heart, until after much prayer and fasting over the matter, he like Paul decided to obey God and "go unto the Gentiles."

After getting the privilege of cleaning up and repairing an old house in Santa Barbara, for its use one year, we moved in and opened it up for a Faith Mission in Spanish.

The first night the devil tried to frighten us out by telling us that the Mexicans would kill us if we attempted to preach to them: but we got a real victory over him in this by placing our lives on the altar for the gospel in Mexico, receiving the answer from the Lord that we should have our lives for a prey.

From that time on we have served the Lord on this line without fear, and God has protected us through dangers seen and unseen, to him be all the praise.

A brother loaned us a Spanish grammar and a New Testament in Spanish. With these we commenced to learn the language. The burden of learning the language was so heavy upon us that we cried mightily to God to help us, and before the first week was ended we went out on the street, preached in Spanish to as attentive an audience as we had ever had. In the fall of this year we felt led of the Lord to go into Lower California, Mexico, to preach there. The Lord had put into our hands money enough to pay our fare to Los Angeles. It was clear that it was the will of God. That night we needed some milk for supper but if I bought milk would not have enough to pay the fare. I told no one of this but at the request of the others I took the pitcher and went out to buy, praying all the time if it was the Lord's will for us to go that I might not be able to get the milk. I went to every place where I knew they had milk but could not get a drop. I went home secretly rejoicing, then I revealed to them what was in my heart.

One of the number volunteered to accompany us to Mexico. So in the morning we very soon arranged all our business matters, which were very few, and at train time we were on board and ready to start on our journey to Mexico. At Los Angeles we had the precious privilege of meeting with and hearing preach for a while dear Brother D. S. Warner and afterward of accompanying him to San Diego.

The time came when we felt the Spirit of the Lord urging us onward in our mission southward. Although we still lacked the means and the steamer was due to start that evening for Ensenada, Lower California, at nine o'clock, we had the assurance that the Lord would provide. We asked a transfer man to come and get our trunks which he did. Then we took our leave of the brethren. In taking our leave of Brother Warner he looked me full in the face and said, ''how much is your fare on the boat?'' I told him. He said, ''Do you lack any of that amount; if so, how much?'' We told him we lacked two dollars. He quietly slipped the two dollars in my hand. Others also in parting with us gave us some so that when we landed at Ensenada we had, I believe, three or four dollars Mexican money. This was our first experience in a foreign country, yet here we found quite a large percent of the population English-speaking people, but under the Mexican rule.

In Ensenada the Methodist sect had a preacher at that time preaching in English but nothing was being done in the Spanish language and nothing has been done since in the Spanish language to our knowledge outside what the Lord us used in a humble way to do.

We rented a small upstairs room at $1.00 per week. This was the best we could do both on account of our limited means and also no rooms were to be had in other parts. The M.E. preacher gave us liberty to preach in his little chapel in English for a few nights, until one of his members began to seek God for a clean heart, and then he concluded he wanted to use the house himself. In the meantime our finances ran out and then a test of our faith came. The brother who came with me was on the point of returning home going afoot overland to San Diego. I expressed my determination to stay and trust God to supply the needs according to the promise; meanwhile I was praying to the Lord not to let us be tempted above what we were able to bear. We continued to call from house to house, talking and praying with the people. When we were entirely out and began to feel the need of food, a Mexican woman handed us a dollar. We truly praised God and took courage. We began to feel that it would be for the glory of God that we push on south into the country around about. We mentioned this to some of the leading ones. The M.E. woman who was seeking a pure heart and another American lady fitted us up with a good supply of food and a little money, while a good-natured Swiss man loaned us a donkey and in a short time we were packed up and ready for a forward march over the country toward the south.

# India

## by

## G. P. Tasker

Excerpted from "Brief History of Our Church of God Work in India Up to the Year 1923" (Unpublished Paper).

# A Time to Remember: BEGINNINGS

**IT ALL BEGAN** in 1893, with the conversion to Christ of an earnest Mohammedan youth of sixteen, named Alaud'din Khan, who was then at school in Mymensingh, East Bengal, and also with keen interest attending a Bible class conducted by a Miss Ehrenburg, of the Australian Baptist Mission, which was working in that district.

The story of this brother's baptism, followed by his kidnapping by fanatical Muslim relatives, who kept him in close confinement for twenty-five days, doing everything in their power to recover him to his former faith, is indeed a thrilling one. Finding their efforts foiled by the wisdom given the boy in replying to all their arguments, they finally sought to spoil his brain, and even to kill him, by putting some of their powerful native poisons into his food. God protected him from harm, even as he did Paul when bitten by the viper. Finally they stopped and let him return to school. In such ways, as we can now see so clearly, the Lord showed that Khan was a chosen vessel unto Him whose life was to have some special meaning in the work of the Church in India.

Another significant fact in this connection is that from the very start of his Christian life Brother Khan decided to believe and to practice only those things which, by a diligent study of the Bible and prayer, he would be enabled to see were clearly taught in the New Testament. It is therefore not surprising that he was soon led into an experience of the Spirit-filled life and a perception of the great truth of the spiritual oneness of all who really are "in Christ." Other important truths, such as the continuing gifts and leadership of the Spirit in the Church which is Christ's body and of which He is the absolute Lord in all things, were made clear to him; with the result that, as he himself wrote, he "became peculiar" and unable to "join" any of the existing denominational churches of the day, though wishing to have full spiritual and cooperative fellowship with all born-again souls wherever he found them.

While attending college in Calcutta he discussed these things with other Christian students, some of whom became favorable to his views. Among these was a young man named Mosir Moses, who was also a convert from Islam, and with whom he continued in prayer and Bible study, despite the reproaches and petty persecutions of some of their more formal Christian friends.

During this time two other important things occurred. He met Mr. R. N. Mundul of Calcutta who was a man of kindred mind, one of whose daughters he finally married. Two other daughters (Sanat and Nalini) later became valued workers in the Shelter, a home for the rescue and protection of minor girls. This home was established in Cuttack in 1915, under Brother Khan and Sister E. Faith Stewart and helpers, at the earnest solicitation of a local Hindu gentleman. "Father Mundul," as he was affectionately known to all of us, died there in 1936 at the most unusual age of 104 years.

The other important event was his happening to see in some paper an advertisement to the effect that a man in Texas was offering, for a dime, to send to anyone samples of holiness literature published in America. As he was deeply interested in the subject of Christian holiness, Brother Khan at once sent the money and in due time received a package of the papers, among them being a copy of the Gospel Trumpet Publishing Company's catalogue of books!

Reading there of such works as *Divine Healing of Soul and Body, Salvation: Present, Perfect, Now or Never,* and *The Church of God: What It Is, and What It Is Not,* he sent for these and was delighted to find in them the very things the Lord had been teaching him in his own private study of the Bible. And this was the beginning of our acquaintance with him and his work—a growingly intimate spiritual and cooperative fellowship which continued to the day of his lamented death in Calcutta over 25 years later, on October 8, 1922.

Twice our brother visited the churches in America: once in 1903-04, and again in 1908-10. His visits greatly increased our missionary interest and strengthened the spiritual ties between us.

It was after his first visit that E. E. Byrum, then editor of the *Gospel Trumpet,* the G. W. Baileys of Washington, and Evalyn Nichols of Idaho returned with him to India. Mr. Byrum stayed for a short time while Mr. Bailey stayed for a whole year.

Evalyn Nichols finally married James J. N. Roy of Assam. Mr. Roy shared the same religious views as Mr. Khan. At this time, 1902, there were standing with Roy only about fifteen of his own Khassi people, but today they number in the thousands.


# Jamaica

### by

### Frederick G. Smith


Excerpted from *Look on the Fields* (Anderson, Ind.: Missionary Board of the Church of God, 1920).

**OUR MISSIONARY** work in Jamaica was opened in 1907 by Brother and Sister George and Nellie Olson, and they have been very successful in their work.

Sister Nellie Olson has written a brief sketch of the work in Jamaica, and I cannot do better than to quote from her:

"It was in the summer following the earthquake of January, 1907, that, in obedience to the leadings of the Spirit of God, we first came to Jamaica. We landed in Port Antonio on the morning of July 29, but not feeling that that was where God would have us we took another ship and came around the island to Kingston, reaching here the following day. Kingston was still in a wrecked condition, heaps of brick, twisted zinc, and tangled wires were everywhere, for the work of reconstruction had not yet begun. But still we felt at home, and happy. A young man who had been a subscriber for the *Gospel Trumpet* and who at that time was selling the Trumpet Company's literature helped us to find a furnished cottage, and we began housekeeping the same day. Earthquake shocks were frequent; the season was very hot, for we were now in the tropics; the people were strange to us; and we had much to learn before we could hope to get to work, so for the first months, and I might say for two years, we were merely laying a foundation for our labors.

"Six months after we came, we were joined by Brother A. S. McNeil, a native Jamaican whom we had met in Anderson, Indiana, and who had embraced the doctrines of the church of God. We were very glad for his able assistance, and God blessed our work together. Before he came, we had gathered about us a few souls who were willing to walk in the Bible way, and with this little congregation here in Kingston our work began."

# Japan

## by

### Frederick G. Smith

Excerpted from *Look on the Fields* (Anderson, Ind.: Missionary Board of the Church of God, 1920).

**OUR MISSIONARY** work in Japan dates from the year 1909 when Brother J. D. Hatch and Brother W. G. Alexander and wife and daughter, Grace, went there as missionaries. Prior to that time Brother A. U. Yajima, a converted Japanese, visited this country and was used of the Lord in building up among us an active interest in the work of the gospel in Japan.

Brother Hatch remained in Japan until 1916, when he was taken seriously ill. An effort was made to bring him back to the United States before his death. He reached California in May, but died shortly afterward.

The Alexanders labored in Japan for more than ten years before taking a furlough, Brother Yajima being a faithful helper. They located at a town named Musashi Sakai, in Tokyo Fu, about fifteen miles west of Tokyo, the capital of the empire. Here Brother Alexander secured about two acres of land and built a private home, which became a sort of missionary home when other workers were kindly admitted.

Immediately adjoining Brother Alexander's property on the

west is a commodious mission house, chapel, and printing plant combined. This building was also erected by Brother Alexander. Here Brother Yajima and his family live, together with the other workers in the publishing plant. The chief periodical is the *Pure Gospel,* published monthly in Japanese. With the regular edition of the paper is run a supplement designed for non-Christians. The plant also publishes tracts and can issue booklets up to ninety-six pages. Brother Yajima is editor of these publications, and in addition does pastoral work.

In 1917 Sister Zuda Lee Chambers went to join our force in Japan and she has become a very efficient worker and is highly respected by the Japanese who know her, as well as by all others. Brother John D. Crose and wife also sailed in 1919.

# Kenya

## by

## Mabel Baker

Excerpted from *Fiftieth Year Jubilee of the Church of God in East Africa: 1905-1955* (Kisumu, Kenya: National Pentecostal Press, 1955).

**ONE OF THE** missionaries in the South African Compounds Mission, which was started in 1896 by Mr. A. W. Baker to evangelize the Africans working in the gold mines around Johannesburg, was a Mr. Robert Wilson. He was a well-seasoned missionary, a sign-writer, rough carpenter, and a bit of a mason. He had a good knowledge of Zulu and a fair one of Sesuto. His wife also spoke Zulu fluently and was a most enthusiastic and energetic helpmeet, with two sturdy sons.

After reading a little magazine called *Hearing and Doing,* published by the Africa Inland Mission, which described pioneer work in British East Africa (now Kenya) and the great spiritual destitution of the people there, Mr. Wilson felt that he was being called of God to go there as a missionary. He spoke to Mr. Baker about this, and was advised to pray earnestly for guidance about it. After some time Mr. Wilson returned to Mr. Baker still burdened as before with the urge to go. Mr. Baker then agreed to pay the expense of a preliminary trip to spy out the land, and see the needs of the people.

On November 17, 1904, Mr. Wilson traveled by train from Johannesburg to Lourenco Marques, and from thence by steamer, arriving at Mombasa on November 29. While ashore at Zanzibar, he saw enough of Mohammedanism to make him long to see the creed of Islam forestalled among the Africans of the interior.

He stayed one night in Mombasa, then proceeded by train to Kijabe. He was received with the greatest cordiality by the Reverend C. S. Hurlburt, director of the Africa Inland Mission. After two days' stay at Kijabe, Mr. Wilson went by rail to Kisumu, the terminus of the railway on Lake Victoria. Kisumu then was only a small place, with a few Indian stores, a couple of forwarding agents, government buildings, and a post office.

The morning after Mr. Wilson's arrival in Kisumu he started out on foot to Kaimosi, the headquarters of the Friends' African Industrial Mission. This mission was then about three years old. The Friends received Mr. Wilson very cordially, and expressed their wish that he should come and labor among the Nyanza people, and indicated the district they thought he ought to occupy. They also very kindly offered to allow him to use their station at Kaimosi as a base of operations until he was settled in his own.

After that, Mr. Wilson returned to South Africa. When the matter of his going came up before the other workers in their mission conference, their decision was unanimous that he and his family should be allowed to go to British East Africa in the name of the mission, which then later became known as the South African Compounds and Interior Mission, to include the new field in the interior.

Accordingly, Mr. and Mrs. Wilson and their family left South Africa and arrived in Kenya, proceeding first to Kaimosi which they made their base for the time being. Trouble began in the

Nandi territory adjoining that of Kaimosi, and the authorities advised the missionaries to move their wives and children away from Kaimosi for a while. The Church Missionary Society had begun a station at Maragoli, and the Reverend Willis was in charge there. He kindly offered the Kaimosi missionaries a haven at Maragoli, and some of them moved there temporarily. Mr. and Mrs. Wilson also accepted this hospitality. While there, Mr. Wilson and Reverend Willis decided to make a tour of inspection together. They went from Maragoli, through Bunyore, and on to the Yala River, which they crossed on a raft made of four empty casks, and thence on to Mumias and beyond. Reverend Willis went on still farther exploring, but Mr. Wilson turned back and returned alone. He passed through Bunyore again, and saw the Chief, Otieno. He found that he was friendly, and favored the idea of the building of a mission in his area.

On August 15, 1905, Mr. and Mrs. Wilson with their children and Baganda porters, and a tent and sufficient food to last a few days, left Maragoli, and moved over to the site in Bunyore which was later called Kima, which is a nickname of Mrs. Wilson. They began at once to build houses of poles and grass for the porters, and for stores. Mrs. Wilson was kept busy buying bundles of grass from the people with salt, and Mr. Wilson bought poles with rice. At first, the Bunyore women and girls were very timid; the slightest move of the Europeans in their direction made them flee and disappear like frightened deer.

August 20, 1905, was the missionaries' first Sunday in Bunyore. They put on different clothes, as they wished to teach the people about Sunday, and when the people brought bundles of grass to sell as usual, they did not buy it, but said that it was God's special day. Seeing about a dozen people standing by, Mr. Wilson asked his wife to sing and play on her small harmonium. As soon as she began to do so, in no time there were about one hundred people in the group. Subsequently, Mr. Wilson used to hang up a white flag on a Sunday to distinguish it from the other days.

The missionaries felt very handicapped at first not knowing

the vernacular, but in due time, with their good background of Zulu, and the help of Mr. Rees' tentative Luragoli vocabulary, they acquired a working knowledge of the language. Singing was very popular with the people, and one of the first hymns which the missionaries taught them was "Jesu akulanga"—"Jesus Is Calling You."

After Mr. and Mrs. Wilson left, Mr. and Mrs. Richardson took charge, and they built a solid foundation for the work. In 1911 Mr. Richardson baptized the first two converts, one of whom was Johana Owenga, who after John Bila's death, carried on his work of preaching. In 1912, there was a second baptismal service when Mr. Richardson baptized thirteen converts. The people liked Mr. Richardson and they called him "Ndeta." When the time came for Mr. and Mrs. Richardson to go on furlough, they asked Mr. and Mrs. Kramer to take charge of the work in their absence.

When Mr. and Mrs. Kramer went on furlough to America, they left Mr. and Mrs. Keller in charge of the work. Mr. Baker and the Council, then in charge of the South African Compounds Mission, asked them to try to find some really evangelistic society there to take over the work of the mission in Kenya. Mr. and Mrs. Kramer suggested the Church of God Missionary Board of Anderson, Indiana, and this suggestion was approved, and the mission then passed into their hands. This was in 1922, and this Board has carried on the work liberally and effectively ever since.

# INDEX

**120**